Letting People Go

Letting People Go

The People-Centered Approach to Firing and Laying Off Employees

Matt Shlosberg

First published in 2010 by
Business Expert Press, LLC
222 East 46th Street, New York, NY 10017
www.businessexpertpress.com

ISBN-13: 978-1-60649-207-9 (paperback)

ISBN-13: 978-1-60649-208-6 (e-book)

DOI 10.4128/9781606492086

A publication in the Business Expert Press Human Resource Management and Organizational Behavior collection

Collection ISSN: 1946-5637 (print)
Collection ISSN: 1946-5645 (electronic)

Cover design by Jonathan Pennell
Interior design by Scribe, Inc.

First edition: November 2010

10 9 8 7 6 5 4 3 2 1

Printed in Taiwan

Note

All ideas published in this book should be taken as opinions. Readers should make their own judgments when following advice they read in this book. Neither publisher nor author are responsible for the effectiveness of content contained in this book and for any damages caused when following any advice contained herein. By reading this book, you agree to hold the author and the publisher harmless in any lawsuits.

Dedicated to people who made a difference in my life.

Abstract

If you manage people, you are probably responsible for firing them. The central message of this book is that layoffs and firings have to be done right. Layoffs and firings do happen. It's just the way business is done. But many companies mishandle terminations, resulting in lawsuits, mass employee exodus, theft, loss of productivity, brand destruction, and many other sicknesses. This book addresses both layoffs and firings and describes how to perform them correctly. It also addresses the role leadership plays in terminations and teaches readers how to have tough conversations.

Keywords

at will employment, firing, laid off, laying off, layoff, letting go, outplacement, termination, terminations

Contents

About the Author

History is written by the victors.

—Winston Churchill

Matt Shlosberg is one of the most sought-after management consultants. He has assisted dozens of multinational corporations and governments with solving complex management problems, resulting in a multibillion-dollar impact.

Matt currently serves as the managing director of Hanna Concern, a management consulting firm specializing in general management, strategy, leadership, organizational behavior, innovation management, marketing, and globalization.

In addition to consulting, Matt teaches leadership, general management, and innovation management in corporate universities.

Matt has received his MBA from the University of Maryland at College Park (Robert H. Smith School of Business) and has completed graduate- and executive-level trainingin leadership and executive management at Cornell University, University of Notre Dame, and INSEAD Business School.

Preface

The central message of this book is that layoffs and firings have to be done right. Layoffs and firings do happen. It's just the way business is done. But many companies mishandle terminations, resulting in lawsuits, mass employee exodus, theft, loss of productivity, brand destruction, and many other sicknesses.

The first chapter of the book addresses just that—why terminations should be executed correctly. The second and third chapters talk about firings and layoffs respectively, explaining how they should be handled. The fourth chapter gives you more food for thought by discussing some complex circumstances and provides some generic advice.

Although each chapter of the book can be read on its own, it's important to use a systemic approach. It's not enough to follow individual pieces of advice addressed in this book. Instead, readers should create a system or a process of talent management, build everything they learn into it, and make sure all the pieces talk to each other.

It's important to remember that this book addresses the management portion of terminations and only barely touches the legal aspects. Because every country and every state has its own set of laws, companies should consult their attorneys before implementing any advice they find in this book.

One of the key notions introduced in this book is the concept of aggravations. These aggravations arise from terminations being performed incorrectly and result in devastating consequences. Although aggravations aren't mentioned in every part of the book, avoiding them is the central strategy discussed here.

I've spent over a decade providing management advice to global firms. It's always been my policy to keep all engagements confidential, and I have never broken this rule. This book features stories and examples from some of my clients. Although many of them are well-known firms, I purposefully suppressed any company and employee names in order to comply with this privacy policy.

If you are still wondering why you should read this book, please read the fun case below. It seems absurd, but cases like this do happen.

An employee quit abruptly and sued the company for sexual harassment, stating she didn't really quit voluntarily but was forced into the position where any reasonable person would quit. She stated sexual harassment was expressed when she saw two male employees kissing in the hallway. She thought it was inappropriate and felt uncomfortable working in such a firm. She won the lawsuit for both sexual harassment and, believe it or not, wrongful termination. But this is just the beginning of the story. Following the court's decision that this is construed as sexual harassment, the company asked the two male employees to not kiss again in public. The two employees sued the company for discrimination and won under the premise that the firm was discriminating against gay personnel.

It sounds crazy. But you wouldn't believe how many times I've heard this from customers only to have them call me later and ask for help in dealing with crazy cases like this. Crazy cases seem rare until they happen to you. But they do happen to the best of us.

The point of the book is to prevent such cases from occurring. If you want to learn how to do that, read on.

—Matt Shlosberg

CHAPTER 1

The Firing Squad

Introduction

The moment I sat down and started to write this book, I received a phone call from a friend who is the founder and chief technology officer (CTO) of the number-one company in his field. He called to tell me that he was about to lay off four vice presidents. He asked me if I could use one of them in my firm. He proceeded to give me a great recommendation on the person he was referring. He had recognized that it was the chief executive officer's (CEO's) mistake in hiring these people in the first place—he knew the reorganization was coming and these positions would be eliminated.

At first I was impressed. He did two things most executives don't do when they let people go: he recognized the source of this mistake and he was trying to help these people find jobs.

But then I got startled. His vice presidents, the very top people he was about to let go, didn't know they were going to lose their jobs the very next day. They knew nothing about the impending financial reorganization. They didn't know their firm was in financial danger. Frankly, some of them didn't even know what their role was. If his VPs were unaware of company issues, what did it say about rank-and-file employees?

As my friend continued, he alarmed me even more. Neither he nor the CEO was going to personally get involved in the layoff. Nor was it delegated to Human Resources (HR)! In fact, his head of HR was laid off just two months earlier under the premise that HR isn't a needed function at all. The CEO decided that this layoff was a financial function. The chief financial officer (CFO) was appointed to run the firing squad.

I can almost predict what will happen next. These executives will get offended. Some may file lawsuits. Others will call the lucky ones that kept their jobs and breed doubt into the organization. The surviving employees will wonder what happened to their peers. People on the bottom will lose trust in senior leadership, spread rumors, and start looking for jobs. Productivity will become a concept of the past. Customers will no longer matter. A wave of negativity will slowly grow into a cancer that will eat this ultrainnovative organization and feed it for lunch to competition.

Does this sound familiar?

Most leaders don't recognize what goes on in people's heads when layoffs and firings occur. A lot of them don't see problems even when these problems are clearly shown to them. In fact, most managers believe that firings and layoffs are just unpleasant things in life that must be done and gotten over with. What they don't realize is that poor execution of layoffs and firings destroy their organizations, often making them even worse off than they were before!

Let's look back at the case I just described. We can point out a lot of things that went wrong, but it's too late to change anything. Well-executed layoffs start early and begin with great leadership coming from the top. This particular organization has built a great legacy. Its product is embedded in over 300 consumer goods that are used by tens of millions of people around the world. But this legacy will get destroyed with a cancer that was essentially produced by the same leadership that created this legacy in the first place.

Remember the old saying "Every system is perfectly designed to achieve exactly the results it gets"? In other words, if this organization gets destroyed, it will happen because the leadership acted the way it did and not because the recently departed staff became disgruntled.

I've worked and consulted for dozens of organizations over the years and the pattern seems steady. Senior leadership mismanages layoffs and then blames organizational failure on employees who became disgruntled for some unknown reason. Sometimes leaders don't even notice the behavioral transformation and manage dysfunctional organizations. One CEO that went through rounds of layoffs concluded in a conversation with me that all people are incompetent. He now spends 95% of his time managing emergencies. Growth, good customer service, loyalty, and faith in leadership are unknown concepts in his organization. Management of this so-called incompetence became such a routine task for him that he no longer recognizes that his organization can behave any differently. He isn't managing change. He is reactively managing daily operations.

Another example I've seen is perhaps the extreme illustration of layoffs hurting the firm. Years ago, I was a consultant for a global firm headquartered in Norway. Located in Baltimore, our unit was in charge of development of one of the firm's key products and was led by the firm's CTO. One day, a senior executive from Norway arrived in our office for a tour. He walked around, introduced himself, and gave us a beautiful speech about the future of the firm. He also told us that he wanted to set up a global product testing center in our facility. This center would be responsible for the testing of all products produced by the firm around the world. He left everyone excited about the future. A week after he left, the VP of marketing for the United States showed up in our office. He gathered everyone in the cafeteria and announced that our guest from a week ago was unimpressed with what he saw and our unit was being shut down. He told the staff that everyone will be laid off within a week or two. He then asked employees to pack all company belongings, inventory them, and deliver them to another company facility located in Virginia.

What do you think employees did? Not a single one continued to perform work! Young staffers spent the remainder of their tenure playing video games. The more experienced crew and folks with families spent time looking for jobs. Managers didn't care to control anyone. They were busy seeking jobs for themselves. One manager took the initiative to rent a truck and deliver the company belongings to the other office, as promised. However, half of the company hardware managed to disappear from the truck and later found itself for sale on the internet or in other employees' homes.

So what went wrong here? This employer thought the layoff was handled properly. People were given a two-week notice. But employees saw something different. First, the gentleman from Norway lied. As a result, employees lost trust in senior leadership. Second, they wanted a senior leader from Norway to come and explain to them what happened. This was a manufacturing unit and they wanted a manufacturing executive to perform the layoff. Instead, they were let go by a junior executive from another division. This seemed like a spit in their faces. Third, they were expected to help the company move its belongings. They felt like this company hadn't been loyal to them, but they were expected to stay loyal to the company. Finally, there was no explanation, no severance, no assistance with job finding, no senior leadership to mentor the upset personnel, and no sign of the CTO, who was quietly laid off the night before the announcement.

Things That Go Wrong: The Importance of Doing It Right

Companies don't let staffers go just because they feel like it. They typically do so to correct a problem or to improve the bottom line. Regardless of the reasons, companies have positive end goals in mind.

But what are some of the things that can go wrong? Experience shows that there can be a myriad of things.

Unemployment costs. Most companies believe they will save money when they let people go. But a lot of them spend more money on employee termination than payroll. One telecommunications company spent millions in legal fees when its terminated employees suspected they were let go due to age discrimination. A large car parts manufacturer was hit with huge early retirement costs when it laid off a part of its workforce. A large technology company paid out huge severance packages equivalent to a six months' salary when it let people go before the economic downturn only to rehire them two months later.

Opportunity costs. Sometimes you will find that reduction in demand for your product will result in reduction in resources needed to execute. This can be a good reason to reduce your staff. If that's the case, go for it! But every now and then companies lay people off without realizing how this reduction in workforce will impact the business. The truth is that every company should be lean. If it is lean, it should never be able to find people to lay off. If it's easy for the firm to identify thousands of people it can do without, these people shouldn't have been working for the firm in the first place. *Great companies should lay off during good economic times, not when things go bad.* I witnessed an example in early 2002 when a telecommunications company laid off a large number of its customer service staff. A financially oriented CEO was hoping that customers wouldn't notice that their on-hold time with customer service went from 0 to 5 minutes. Not only did customers notice; they left. Another great example I've seen recently is where a large shopping mall operator decided to reduce layers of management and lay off its operations managers, replacing them with regional managers. The idea seemed great. The company saved tons of money on payroll. But people that made this decision didn't understand how this move would impact operations. The old hands-on, financially savvy, community-oriented operations managers knew customers, kept them happy, made sure malls ran smoothly, and ensured occupancy was high and malls were profitable. The new guys knew nothing about operations or finance, didn't know customers, were spread too thin managing several malls, didn't know their own staff or what was expected of them, didn't understand the overall mission, and didn't know how to execute. Not only did they miss the how, but they were demoted in their own minds when they took new positions and had absolutely no desire to make anything happen. Their staff saw the reduction in performance of their leaders and followed suit. Cost savings went away. So did customer service. One mall I studied increased its operating cost by over a million dollars per year after reducing its payroll by $150,000.

Employee stress. Most companies don't care about stress of outgoing employees, but this stress can kill the very company that let them go. Stressful employees are known to call the peers who stayed behind and plant doubt into the organization. They can sue and spend countless hours and dollars in unemployment and legal hearings. They spread the word to their friends and the company's brand slowly dies. Customers stop buying. Potential employees don't apply for future jobs. I've heard one senior executive complain that she couldn't find people to work for her. Prospective employees heard so much negativity about the firm that they'd rather stay unemployed than work for this organization.

Negative action. This can be expressed in a lot of ways. From stolen company property to objects flying in bosses' faces, from broken car windows to lawsuits, people react and this reaction can cause you money and stress.

Remaining employees. This is the most obvious and most important weakness in the organization. Yet most employers tend to ignore it. When people get laid off, the remaining employees always ask the same questions: "What happened? Why a lay off? Why them? Why not me? Is this the end of it? Will there be more? When will I be laid off? What is the risk?"

If no one can answer their questions, they start speculating. Speculation turns into rumors, and the rumor mill has no limits. Whatever they decide, the end result is always the same—it's time to look for another job. Some employees leave. Others start looking for opportunities. All of a sudden, money becomes less of an object than it was when they first accepted the job. They all look for stability. This search for a new job becomes their new purpose in life. Their regular job no longer exists. Neither does productivity. This remaining workforce turns into a slow-moving, careless liability. People who were once considered stars create the basis for not doing their work: "It doesn't matter anymore. I'll get laid off soon anyway." These words will come from the same people you considered for promotion just weeks earlier. But wait! They will go many steps further! First, they will let their friends know to not accept a job with your firm. Why? Because they'll get laid off as soon as they join! Then your stars will become heavily stressed and sometimes go into depression. They will use it as justification for poor performance and they'll strongly believe in the validity of their excuse. They will call the employees that just left to exchange their stress. Although they expect that they'll feel better after such conversations, they usually become stressed even more. Your customer service people will talk to customers with a sigh instead of a smile. Your demotivated customer retention team will work to lose customers. All of a sudden, people will start taking vacations and sick days (of course, they need to interview!), raising your fringe benefit rate and reducing work coverage and productivity. The bottom line is that work will no longer exist in your organization.

As you can see from the previous examples, termination of employees can harm the organization in both the long term and the short term. If companies have positive goals, they have to do whatever it takes to prevent any harm to the organization. That's why layoffs and firings should be done correctly.

Horrors of the Firing Squad

I hate to compare letting people go with killing them. Of course these are two different things! Luckily, firings don't typically result in deaths. But history shows many cases where lost jobs took people to extremes no one ever thought possible.

Consider the following examples.

Example 1

Some time ago, I interviewed a gentleman for a junior manager position. He interviewed well. He possessed great functional knowledge and had great leadership skills. He looked like a star. But there were two things that surprised me. First, this highly paid individual was unemployed for an extended period of time, which seemed unusual for his position, especially given the exceptionally great market conditions. Second, I noticed that he lived in low-income housing, where payment in cash was required for rent every month up front. This combination surprised me. I ran his background check per company policy and found two issues. One, he had a dishonorable discharge from the military. Two, he had a felony on his record. Per state law, I disclosed the findings to him and heard the horror story as a reply. This young man made a mistake when he was in the army. It wasn't a big deal; he probably would have kept his job if he was in the private sector. But he was discharged, or, in the words of the private sector, fired. This discharge went into his record and haunted him for the rest of his life. He couldn't get a job. This highly skilled individual was left on the street while his wife was staying at home with a newborn baby. He spent many months looking for another job until he found one. A few months later he got laid off. By the time I met him, he was unemployed for over a year. He went into a heavy depression. How could he take care of his family if he couldn't find a job? He moved into low-income housing, but he couldn't afford to pay for it. He told me he had plenty of interviews, and he heard good feedback from potential employers, but the process would always stop when his potential employer heard of his termination from the military.

Unfortunately I wasn't in the position to hire him either. I felt bad for him. This extremely capable individual ruined his whole life by getting fired from the army. His story also explained the felony on his record. He got caught stealing. But he didn't do it because he was a bad person. He was a desperate person trying to feed his family.

I have a friend who used to be a fatalities-processing clerk in the military. He told me he used to process one suicide per week that either current or ex-military personnel committed due to their financial problems.

Example 2

I met a manager who was laid off from a major diversified technology-services firm. This individual was highly competent. He was a successful serial entrepreneur and worked as a senior executive for a variety of companies. He wasn't worried when he lost his job. It seemed like he could find another one quickly. But things didn't turn out the way he wished. It took him almost three years to find another job. He went into a heavy depression. His wife tried to commit suicide and then spent time in a mental institution. When she came back, she filed for divorce and took away his life's savings. In turn, he stole money from his business partner so he could survive. As in the previous case, this man justified his theft because he needed the money to survive. He lost lots of friends as well as his reputation, which he may never recover.

Example 3

I used to play in bands when I was younger. The rock 'n' roll scene exposed me to the world of individuals who had low-paying jobs as a way to survive while they played music with hopes of making it big someday. I remember I met an excellent drummer. He was laid off from his job after having spent 15 years there. The day he got laid off, he drove home fast so he could see his wife and relax from the stress of unemployment in the comfort of his home. He was pulled over by police for speeding, and the officer suspended his license. He desperately tried to look for another job, but he couldn't even go to an interview—he could no longer drive. One day he took the risk and drove to an interview. After all, he didn't have a choice. He had a family to feed. His wife was handicapped after a car accident and couldn't work, so she stayed home with their two kids. As he drove to the interview, he got pulled over by police. He was arrested for driving with a suspended driver's license. The judge gave him 30 days in prison and suspended his driver's license for 3 years.

This individual felt like he was put in front of the firing squad.

So What?

It seems like these three examples show the extremes of what happens. But here's what we should all think about: According to a survey conducted by CareerBuilder, 47% of all Americans live paycheck to paycheck.[1] This means that 47% of the population doesn't have any savings. If that's the case, then this means, of the 47% of the people who live paycheck to paycheck, those who lose their jobs may have problems similar to the ones we described in our extreme cases. Most of these cases will be closer to example 2, but all three cases may occur. So maybe these cases are not that extreme.

I am sure your first question is "So what? Just because they don't know how to save money doesn't mean we shouldn't let them go." You are absolutely right. If you need to let them go, then go for it. But you should make sure to do it correctly. Look at the introduction to this chapter that talks about the why. Then think about these extreme examples we just discussed. What do you think people can do to your organization if put in this position? What would you do if your organization put you on the street with no savings? Now consider the fact that this happens to at least 47% of the people! The other 53% of the people get impacted as well. They may survive for a little longer than the unlucky bunch that didn't save money, but they will face the same challenge if they don't find a job soon.

Think about it this way. When you let them go, it won't be about them as much as it will be about your organization! Therefore, it is essential to control the process. One way to control it is to help the people you let go.

There are many possibilities for helping these people. The following chapters will give you lots of ideas on the types of things you can do.

Here's a teaser example.

I have a great friend who is a division CEO of a multibillion-dollar firm. He told me that his firm lost a large contract to a major competitor. As a result, the company had to let 120 people go. But what his firm did was extraordinary. Instead of letting staff go, the company called the competitor that just took its contract away and asked if they could use the people. One phone conversation between senior executives saved 80 out of 120 jobs. These 80 people got transferred to the new organization. Then the company found jobs for 20 of the ones that were left in other divisions of the firm and gave large severance checks to the 20 it had to let go. Employees were very thankful. Everyone understood the challenge. Those who lost their jobs were well prepared by the firm in advance and received enough cash to survive for a few months. The firm organized the layoff so well that these people didn't feel the impact of losing their jobs. To them, it felt more like a logical transition to the next project. The layoff went pretty much unnoticed. Those who were displaced thought the firm took care of them.

Employees Versus Contractors

Near the beginning of my consulting career, I worked for a global IT consulting firm. This firm grew quickly. It had 5,000 employees when I joined and over 6,000 employees only 6 months later. As a consultant, I was expected to provide technical services on long-term contracts to Fortune 1000 clients. Although I was clearly told who I was working for and I knew exactly who gave me my paycheck, I never felt like I was a part of this consulting organization. I switched clients three times during my tenure with the consulting firm. But I always felt like I was a part of my client's team and I felt like my client was my employer!

Owners of consulting firms specializing in long-term projects don't usually see this. They believe in employee loyalty and think that their staff embraces their culture. But this culture is virtual; there's no culture to embrace! It doesn't matter if they are employees or contractors. They are humans first! When humans enter an organization, they see, believe in, and buy into the culture of their clients. They don't see the culture of companies providing their paychecks, but they go to lunch with their clients, participate in their meetings, go to their corporate events, abide by their processes and procedures, and communicate with their staff. They do things the way their clients want them done, not the way their consulting firm dictates.

When I worked for this consulting firm, I was told that we were great for being International Organization for Standardization (ISO) 9001[2] registered, having great career opportunities and top-notch people. But as a consultant working at the client's site, I had no idea what ISO 9001 meant, I had no idea how I could explore great career opportunities that supposedly existed, and I'd never met any of the top-notch people working on other customers' sites. I never knew who my boss was, but I did work for various managers at clients' sites whom I always regarded as my bosses. When my contract engagements were over, I was devastated. I knew in my head that this simply meant the end of the contract period, but in my heart I felt like I was either laid off or fired.

I've seen many similar situations.

My wife worked for a large property management firm. Her job was to assist with the management of a large shopping mall belonging to her client. She spent a year and a half working for the client. She never met any representatives of her employer other than on her initial job interview day. She didn't know where they were located, nor did she care to know. She felt like she was a part of her client's team. When she left, she gave her client a resignation letter, rather than giving it to her employer. Why? She hardly knew who her employer was.

So what's the moral here? If you are a client hiring a consulting firm, you should treat consultants like your own employees! I am not talking about legal aspects of employment.[3] I am talking about leadership. As human beings, consultants need to be motivated just like employees.

Most people think that this is nonsense. After all, that's exactly why they hire consultants. To them, consultants are vendors. They come and go. You don't have to pay them benefits. You don't have to worry about motivating them and dealing with their personal issues. You don't have to consider their feelings. You think they are disposable. You believe they know they are on a contract that will eventually go away.

This is where true leadership comes in. True leaders manage human resources, not employee or consultant resources. And humans have feelings. They want stable jobs. They want to fit in a culture. They like to communicate and feel valuable. But very few consulting companies care to motivate them, and in most cases, these firms can't create a culture consultants can feel a part of simply because consultants never see it.

I've seen many cases where customers wrongfully thought their consultants and vendors were motivated simply because the customer was paying them money. But think about this—just because you buy a burger at McDonald's doesn't mean the cashier is motivated to do his job and cares enough to do it well. Think of your consultant as a cashier in McDonald's. Money has an equal impact on motivation on both of them.

Here's an actual case that I witnessed recently.

A company I was recently advising hired a consulting company to provide it with a couple of senior level engineers. Both were very bright. Both had similar backgrounds and comparable functional capabilities. One was told he was there on a 1-year contract that would be extended for another year if he performed well. The other one was told that his function was that of support, and his contract would be over in 2 to 3 months. The first engineer stayed there for over a year and had an outstanding level of performance. The second one did well for the first three months. After that he asked his client if he was going to stay on the contract for another few months. For a number of reasons, the client refused to answer his question and continued his contract on a day-to-day basis. Obviously unhappy, this consultant went to his consulting firm to see if they could give him an answer, but they couldn't give him any more information, nor did they care to—all they wanted to do was bill the client while they could. The consultant first became demotivated. After all, he saw no purpose in performing any more work if his job was going away. Then he slid into what looked like a heavy depression. "Performance" became a nonexistent word in his vocabulary. He started coming to work late and leaving early, thinking that it didn't matter, since he would be let go soon anyway.

When I brought up this issue with the client, I got a standard response most customers give in such a situation. This client believed that it wasn't her job to motivate the engineer and any performance-related issues were between the engineer and his employer. She further thought that the engineer should be self-motivated because he received a salary he wouldn't receive otherwise if this client didn't hire his firm. But things only look simple! This consultant was simply a human being who wanted to know that his job was stable and he was being valued! His client never gave him any feedback regarding his performance nor did she communicate about his future with the firm. There were no growth opportunities and the short-term outlook didn't look promising. When this consultant became demotivated and his performance dropped, the client simply let this consultant go, giving him a week notice. The client thought she did the right thing—she removed a nonperforming resource and gave his consulting company a whole week to find another engagement for this consultant. What looked like a simple decision turned into a mini disaster. This already aggravated engineer was upset that he was being fired and being given a 1-week notice after asking the customer for many months to give him some kind of an indication about his status with the firm. He went around and told the client's employees, who he now regarded as members of his team, about him being let go with a short notice. Rumors started spreading. People started talking. Soon, everyone decided that the company was starting a set of layoffs. Most people weren't aware that this team member was a consultant and were disgusted with how their firm treated their fellow teammate. They started looking for jobs. The motivation level went down. It took a lot of effort to restore employee trust in the organization.

There are many other examples I can think of where contractor terminations turned into infinite nightmares. Every time it happens, clients make the same mistakes—they treat consultants like disposable goods. They don't treat them like human capital. Although the results are usually not as devastating as situations in which companies let their own employees go, they can create a mess.

Real leaders don't differentiate between contractors and employees in anything other than legal issues. All people deserve the same level of attention and require the same type of leadership techniques to make them effective. Real leaders terminate both employees and contractors the same exact way.

It's About Leadership

By looking at some of the previous sections, you've probably guessed by now that successful employee termination has a lot to do with leadership.

People follow strong leaders anywhere. Leadership can be powerful, but it can also be dangerous. Millions of Germans followed Hitler's directions and killed tens of millions of people. Joseph Stalin successfully led the country after putting 20 million of his own people in prisons. Religious sect leaders convinced their own followers to kill themselves or dedicate their lives to the beliefs of one person. In contrast, against all odds, Gandhi led India to freedom by using his peaceful disobedience methodology.

Imagine how much good charismatic leaders like Stalin and Hitler could have done if they had directed their abilities toward something positive! At the same time, Gandhi could have destroyed more people than

Stalin and Hitler did due to his amazing leadership qualities and the size of India's population.

Letting people go can be implemented in either Hitler's or Gandhi's way and it's up to every leader to determine the strategy he or she will follow. Most companies don't associate themselves with either strategy, but, surprisingly, most terminations look like Hitler's deeds, even if such approach wasn't planned.

I've witnessed one firing of a middle manager in a Fortune 500 firm who simply became a scapegoat of a multimillion-dollar disaster. As a result of an integrity problem that occurred outside of this person's control, this firm was about to lose a contract that was worth hundreds of millions of dollars. In order to save the contract and keep this key customer, his company announced that the problem occurred because of this middle manager's ignorance and terminated him immediately. This manager was a hot commodity. He started getting calls from employers, but no one wanted to hire him once they found out about his adventure at the previous firm. One such firm ran a background check and confirmed that he was fired for an "integrity violation." He eventually found a job, but his reputation will take many more years to restore.

So what went wrong here? His firm knew that there was no violation on his part. To them, it was about money. They didn't think they acted in a Hitler-like way. After all, their actions restored a multimillion dollar contract, although it was done in a Machiavellian way. But they destroyed this human being. Gandhi would probably have done this differently. He would have thanked this employee for his continued contributions and paid him a reasonable severance. He would then personally go out of his way to help this individual find a job.

Federal government contractors in the United States represent another great example. There are thousands of firms in this sector selling business-processing outsourcing services. These companies bid on 2- or 3-year contracts and hire people knowing that these folks will lose their jobs at the contract's end. I've witnessed people leave nice, stable jobs in order to make a little bit more money working for a government contractor only to find out later that their jobs are temporary. When you discuss this dilemma with government contractors, most tell you the same thing— they have to do it! It's the nature of their business. These contractors don't think about their employees. Workers join the firm with happy faces and leave shortly thereafter with stress, hatred, feelings of being betrayed, and tears in their eyes. Government contractors believe that this is the Gandhi way. After all, they give people jobs. But contrary to their beliefs, this looks more like the Hitler way. These people may not necessarily need the jobs that will disappear soon, even if they make more money in the short term. They don't want the stress of looking for another job.

While such practices may seem cruel, they may be the necessary evil in firms with business models that depend on quick hiring and firing of staff. Fortunately, there are ways for these firms to reinvent themselves and follow the Gandhi style of leadership.

Another interesting leadership challenge is the ability to execute strategies at all levels. Gandhi and Stalin were able to execute their plans because they surrounded themselves with great people who believed in their missions and knew how to go about performing their tasks. In turn, these people surrounded themselves with other great people who could also execute their strategies. Leaders' messages resonated well from the very top to the very bottom, and everyone believed in them and wanted to be a part of the success.

This ability to execute plans on all levels is key to successful terminations. It's not enough for the leader to convey the message to his staff. His staff should be able to convey it down to every level. When a company CEO announces a layoff, it doesn't help if only top VPs understand the reasons behind it. The reasons should be communicated down to people on the very bottom of the pyramid. In order to communicate it properly, firms must have leaders at all levels.

Leadership is definitely important. Chapters 2 and 3 of this book focus on the most effective combination of leadership techniques required to let employees go.

Psychology of a Fired Human Being

One of the most common mistakes employers make when terminating employees is to assume that employees understand why they are being let go. What's worse is they sometimes assume that employees are OK with that.

I've been a part of a layoff that occurred due to a merger between two firms. As a result of this merger, the firm was going to lay off several hundred people. The unlucky bunch was gathered in a conference room, and they were told what happened and why they were being let go. This explanation seemed pretty clear and made perfect business sense. But immediately after the meeting, I heard the following statements from employees being terminated:

> "Why would the company terminate our jobs if they have enough money to pay our salaries even if we have no real work to do?"
>
> "I don't know about other people, but I know I am being let go because I am black."
>
> "I am going to sue for wrongful termination. They have no right to lay us off."

The same happens with employee firing. Ask yourself a question. How often do you see scenarios where people understand why they are being fired and they agree with the decision? The challenge with most employers is that firings are usually one-way conversations. An employer would speak and an employee would sit in a state of shock. Managers believe that employees listen just because managers talk, but that's rarely the case.

Of course, there are exceptions. As a matter of fact, we'll discuss them in the next two parts of the book. When followed, these rules will create productive terminations with minimum blood spilled. But what happens in most cases? The following list outlines the framework that represents the person's state of mind when being let go:

1. *Opening remarks.* The employer starts the conversation by giving some background on the situation. While he speaks, the employee runs through some thoughts in his or her head: "Where is my boss going with this? Why am I being told this? Am I being fired? By the way, what did I just hear?"

2. *Pulling the trigger.* The employer makes a statement that the employee is being terminated. The employee is in the state of shock. He or she can't believe what happened and doesn't know what to say.

3. *State of denial.* The employer describes the reasons for termination. The employee disagrees. The employee believes he or she is being set up or misunderstood, or the employee believes the employer is misstating the facts.

4. *Fight back.* The employee tries to argue with the employer and prove him or her wrong. The employee believes the employer is either (a) delusional and simply doesn't know all the facts or (b) unfair. The employee thinks the employer will most likely agree with the arguments presented and will somehow let the employee keep his or her job.

5. *Vengeance.* The employee realizes that there's nothing he or she can do but wants to fight back. The employee's first thoughts include going to a lawyer and suing the employer for a large chunk of money, talking to his or her boss's superior, or coming up with some way to hurt either the person who did the firing or the whole company. The employee often thinks this was personal and believes it had nothing to do with his or her performance.

6. *Waves of frustration.* The employee calms down. Sometimes he or she talks to an attorney and to his or her friends, relatives, or coworkers and tells everyone how he or she was mistreated. At some point the employee realizes there's nothing that can be done to get his or her position back. The employee decides to get the situation over with. He or she will need to process some termination paperwork like benefits, return company keys and equipment, and get his or her final check. The employee's disapproval of the situation comes back. He or she enters the second state of denial. Eventually the employee calms down and forgets about it.

As you can see from this framework, there isn't a second in time when an employee tries to understand why he was let go. There's also no indication that the employee will be OK with this termination decision. What you do see here is the tendency of both parties to argue. Although most people won't call this arguing, it is! In fact, both the employer and the employee present their arguments, which they innocently like to call facts. The employer believes he or she is right to fire the employee, and the employee tries to argue either to convince the employer that he or she is wrong or to file a lawsuit against the employer and prove his or her purity in court.

Yes, this is essentially an argument. But who typically wins an argument like this? No one. Do you remember the last time you won one? The best you can probably recollect is when *you think* you won the argument, but the other party thought he or she won as well.

So if firing conversations are nothing but arguments that can never be won, why would employers spend time and aggravate employees they are about to terminate by telling them stories full of lies, flawed arguments, and deception? Why would employers think they are following the Gandhi approach, doing something good for a company, if they are really hurting innocent employees and terminating their jobs, lives, and dreams in a Hitler-like way?

Remember these things when you read the next part of the book and when you fire employees. Most firings are nothing but arguments that cannot be won. People have feelings. When you fire them, you are fighting against feelings, not logic-based arguments.

CHAPTER 2

Firing

If You Want to Learn More
About Yourself, Fire Someone

One beautiful morning, I got to the office to find my HR department terminating an employee. This firing was terribly mishandled in a lot of ways. The employee was outraged. She stormed out of the conference room, called the HR representative several names I won't repeat in this book, told the confused receptionist she was fat, mentioned to another passing employee that the entire organization had an obesity problem, called an engineer a low-life, picked up her purse, and left.

I asked the HR representative if he learned anything about himself. He nodded in agreement and repeated the foul feedback he had received from the terminated employee just seconds ago.

What looked like a joke at first turned into a great learning exercise. While he added new unclean words to his vocabulary, he also realized how little he knew about letting people go.

Firing is about leadership. When you fire someone, you put your leadership skills to the test. You can do well if you possess great leadership skills. Otherwise, you will get someone to tell you about your obesity problem.

Every time you fire a person, you get a unique opportunity to learn about your leadership abilities. But this opportunity won't force itself in your head. You have to be willing to accept it.

Let's consider the following two examples.

Example 1

One day I received a phone call from a junior manager, let's call her Patricia, who sounded extremely mad. She asked that I come into her office immediately to help her in an emergency situation. When I walked into her office, she was sitting there with Jim, one of her employees, screaming at him. It sounded like a nonstop explosion going off. I couldn't understand what she was screaming about. Jim tried to interrupt Patricia several times to say a few words of defense, but she wasn't listening. She stopped yelling and asked Jim, "Would you want me to fire you, or would you rather resign?" Her employee tried to respond but only got a chance to say, "Hold on, can we talk . . ." when he heard another explosion: "You are fired! Get out now!" The employee stood up, walked out of the office and through an open office area where a dozen or so people stared at him in disbelief (they all heard the boss screaming), and headed for the exit door. After the show was over, I turned to the firing manager and asked why the employee was let go. She now looked like the nicest person in the world. It seems nothing had happened just a moment ago. "Oh, he sent a personal email to his co-worker asking how her day is going," was the reply. "It's against our company policy to send personal emails."

Example 2

My friend, let's refer to him as Joe, received a call from his security officer stating that one of the employees in his organization was spending too much time reading personal email, and his boss wasn't doing anything about it. A similar call went to HR. The HR department came back to Joe immediately with a memo requiring him to give his employee a notice that he will be terminated within 30 days if he doesn't stop reading personal emails. It looked obvious at first—Joe's employee was wasting time doing personal things rather than doing work. But Joe also saw something that he thought no one else could see—a good, typically productive employee with a great attitude and passion to get things done, who was nonproductive and violating a company policy that he was well aware of. Overcoming their resistance, Joe told HR and security he wanted to investigate this further before any write-ups occur. Joe called this employee's manager and asked him what happened. The response he received was even more mysterious. This manager was well aware of the situation, and he wanted to handle it himself, without any involvement from Joe, HR, or security. Joe would normally welcome that; after all, he should empower his employees to deal with their own issues. But his explanation seemed strange. It seemed to Joe that this manager tried to hide what really happened, tried to change the conversation subject, and tried to make the problem hidden from the rest of the world. Something didn't sound right. Normally Joe didn't micromanage, but this situation seemed odd. He was afraid that this employee might end up being a scapegoat. He also didn't hear anything from the manager indicating that he was going to solve the problem. Joe only thought this manager would continue to hide something. Joe called the employee directly. A brief conversation uncovered the problem. His boss, who Joe thought was covering up something, was so busy that he didn't have time to talk to this employee and give him any guidance on the work the employee was supposed to perform. This employee would go to his boss at least once a day and request help. He would also tell his boss that he needed some work assigned to him. The response was always the same—his boss was too busy. Joe called the employee's manager back and told him he would have to let his employee go, hoping this senseless tactic would force this manager to confess. Confess he did. This employee had been asking for guidance for over a month.

These examples have one thing in common—they illustrate leadership failure. The outcomes of these two cases were different, however.

In the first case, the firing manager learned absolutely nothing. It's been years, and she still believes she was right. Her team became extremely demotivated, employee turnover went up to over 100% per year, and quality and innovation were nonexistent concepts. Fortunately, she is no longer there. The new manager reduced the employee turnover rate down to almost zero and introduced many quality initiatives and various innovations that made her organization more productive and more competitive.

In our second case, both Joe and the manager under him learned something. The manager realized that it's his leadership abilities, time management, and overall project-management approach that required improvement. Joe, the executive, realized that he needed to change the coaching approach he used and teach his management team new skills. He also realized his own failure in selecting people, giving them the right tools, and guiding them to do the right thing. Both Joe and the manager below him learned and improved.

*   *   *

Since we are talking about leadership, I'd like to touch on this subject a little bit more. Coaching managers over the years, listening to lectures, and reading dozens of books on leadership, I've heard thousands of definitions of leadership. But there are three concepts I've heard that I like the most.

I heard the first one from Jim Parker, a former CEO of Southwest Airlines. He said that leaders put the right people in the right jobs, communicate their vision, give them a mission, provide tools to execute the vision, coach them, and then get out of their way.

The second one came from Jack Welch, former chairman of General Electric. He talked about the four Es. Leaders should be *energetic*, should be able to *energize* others, should have an ability to *execute* visions, and must have an *edge* to make tough decisions. These Es should be connected by one P—*passion*.

The third one came from Hank Sims, a business professor from the University of Maryland at College Park, and Charles Manz, a business professor from the University of Massachusetts. In their "superleadership"[1] book, they talk about leaders being able to lead people to lead themselves.

These three concepts represent decades of experience. Although this book is not about leadership, everyone in the position of letting people go should consider these concepts before terminating employees. Any time you fire an employee, consider how your leadership skills contributed to employee performance. Very often, managers fail to communicate the mission and the vision, give people the right tools, coach them, or simply stay out of their way, and then they announce "poor performance" as the final verdict and let people go.

Every time you terminate an employee, look back and consider lessons learned. What could you have done to prevent the termination in the first place? Think about this: 75% of the people leave voluntarily because of poor management.[2] This statistic suggests that managers are to blame for a lot of poor performance. In fact, in 75% of the cases poor performance is linked to poor management. Therefore, when you fire employees, consider the fact that there's a 75% chance that they performed poorly because of you.

Learn about yourself every time you terminate an employee!

Misfits, Poor Fits, and Screw-Ups

One of the most important questions employers must ask when firing employees is a simple "Why?" When asked why employers fired people, employers typically break down the why into these two categories:

Screw-ups. These are people who made mistakes or did something out of ignorance that resulted in an unwanted event. Examples may include simple things, like forgetting to turn on the burglar alarm, cheating on a timesheet, getting a major customer upset, or more serious things, such as theft, violence, sexual harassment, and drug use.

Poor performers. These are people who don't necessarily screw anything up but, nonetheless, make employers unhappy for one reason or another. Typical reasons include poor functional knowledge, unwillingness to go the extra mile to perform the task, personality incompatible with company culture, tardiness, ignorance, general human flaws, and many others.

The first category is obvious. You simply have no choice when people make poor decisions. But think about the second one. Every reason listed above states that there's something wrong with the employee. In fact, it says that it's the employee who possesses poor functional knowledge, the employee who doesn't want to go the extra mile, and the employee whose personality doesn't fit the employer's culture. But there's nothing here about the employer!

The reality is people in this category aren't always poor performers. Usually they fall into one of the following two groups.

Group 1: The wrong people in the wrong jobs. Consider the following example. If you hire the best car mechanic and ask him to perform an open heart surgery on a patient, will he fail because he is a poor performer or because he is simply not fit for the job? If you make a hiring decision and your hire doesn't perform as expected, is it his fault that he isn't what you need or is it your fault for hiring him and putting him in this position in the first place?

If we rethink the poor performers category, we can easily reclassify it simply as people who are in the wrong jobs. Regardless of what you may think at first, there's a perfect job for everyone.

I've seen a person with a degree in finance who suffered as an accountant because he wasn't detail oriented. His employer yelled at him and demanded things that this poor soul couldn't deliver. His employer kept on complaining, stating that this accountant was a poor performer. But the trouble is, it's the employer who found this finance expert and hired him in the first place. It's the employer who didn't see the difference between finance and accounting and saw this person as a good fit.

I've also seen a person who was hired by a start-up company that required him to put his heart and soul into the firm and work long, extended hours. But this person was nearing retirement. His heart was with his family. His goal was to have a very easy job, work 8 hours a day, and then go home and spend time with his kids. He wasn't interested in overtime work; he was counting days until retirement. His employer was extremely dissatisfied with his performance. They couldn't get the employee to work extra hours, respond quickly to customers, or to care about the business. His employer wanted to let him go several times for poor performance. But he wasn't a poor performer. He was just a bad fit for the organizational culture that required the long hours and dedication typically required by start-up firms.

As you can see from the previous examples, people aren't evil. Their performance isn't necessarily bad because they want to hurt someone. In fact, the majority of poor performers want to do a good job but can't because they are in the wrong jobs.

Group 2: Poor leadership. Most bosses believe that people are motivated by money. But here are a few thoughts. A recent study performed by Florida State University professor Wayne Hochwarter suggested that 40% of employees believe they work for bad bosses.[3] Other studies conducted by Gallup and mentioned by Leigh Branham in his book The *7 Hidden Reasons Employees Leave*[4] suggest that as many as 75% of people leave their jobs due to bad bosses and 90% leave due to either bad bosses or a bad work environment. Another study asked employees to name 10 things that motivate them. Among the top reasons were things like being able to make a difference, feeling productive and good about the work performed, and having a great team and a great work environment. Money was nowhere on the list.

The top ten reasons come down to one central theme—leadership. I've seen numerous cases of top performers getting demotivated under poor leaders. I've also seen cases of regular people developing passion for mundane work under great leaders.

Consider the following example. My client had a top-performing engineer who spent many years developing numerous products that brought the firm millions of dollars. He was a star and everyone recognized it. One day his boss approached him and asked him to do something this engineer had never done before—maintenance of an existing product. Being an innovator and always wanting to create something new made it tough for this engineer to work on a mundane maintenance project. He took it but asked that someone take over this project as soon as the resources became available. For the next 12 months, this engineer approached his boss and asked if anything had been done to take the project away from him so he could go back to creating and doing what he loved. After a year of hearing negative responses, this engineer lost his motivation. His performance significantly degraded. His interest in work disappeared. So did the extended hours he used to put in. His boss noticed the change in performance but never saw beyond it. The boss never thought for a second that he was the one contributing to this problem. He saw the problem to be that of an employee and not one of his own. The employee ended up quitting and the boss ended up thinking that this employee was incompetent in the first place.

There are many other examples illustrating this concept. Before categorizing an employee as a poor performer, think what you have personally done to contribute to the employee's success and whether or not something could have been done differently.

Here are some candid questions you can ask yourself:

- Did I communicate my vision clearly? Do my employees understand it? Do they see it? How can I prove that they do?
- Did I give them a mission to accomplish? Do they understand the entire mission along with goals and the methodology required to achieve them? Do they agree with it?
- Did I give my employees the tools to execute this vision? Do they have everything they need to do the job effectively? Is there anything they've asked for or they should have asked for that I haven't given them?
- Did I coach my employees? Did they agree with my views? If they didn't agree, what are the implications? Should I reconsider

my views? What if my employee was right and I coached him about something he knows better?

- Did I motivate my employee? Does my employee believe in what we are trying to accomplish? If not, what can I do to change that?
- Did I let my employees execute? Did I get out of their way, or did I micromanage every step?
- What does my employee think of me in general? What have I done to show my employees that I personally care about the work I do?
- Do I show any gratitude for the work being done? In what way? How often? Does my gratitude seem real? Do people think that I care about them? How can I prove it?

If you are truly honest with yourself, answers to these questions may provide you with surprising insights into the performance of your people. You may find that it's your own performance you should be worried about.

* * *

When firing a person, one should always consider the reason for termination and see if it really makes sense. Most people are either poor fits for the job or are poorly led. If you don't think they are a poor fit, consider what you've done to change their situation and whether they should be terminated in the first place.

Where Should People Go Next?

As you can see, people aren't generally evil. Most want to do a good job. Most fall into one of two buckets: poor job fits or poorly led. Neither the poor fits nor the poorly led people are at fault for being placed in their situations. Most have been put in their jobs by their employers. Therefore, if they are laid off or fired, ethics dictate that employers must help them find their next job.

Consider the following example I recently witnessed. An employee found his dream job. It offered a very relaxed atmosphere. He was working no more than eight hours a day. Flexible hours allowed him to spend a lot of time with his family. He had a nice salary and great benefits. Being a government job, this position offered stability, making it possible for the employee to relax and await his retirement, which was coming up shortly. He took the job and worked there for a couple of years. Everything seemed great and nothing could possibly go wrong until one day he received a call from his previous employer. He was offered a job that paid much more money, had even greater benefits, and offered him an opportunity to showcase his skills. Without considering other aspects of his dream job, which he couldn't even see,[5] he took the offer. All would have been fine if this position was a good fit. However, this position required him to work long hours and constantly perform under great pressure. In addition, this job called for him to make tough decisions quickly and work well in a large team environment, which this employee was never trained to do and never cared to be able to do. What seemed like a good idea turned into a disaster. His performance at this new job was far below expectations, putting the company in jeopardy. He ended up being fired for poor performance. From the company's perspective, he was a poor performer. From his perspective, he was stolen away from his dream job by promises of more money, forced to do what he hated doing, and then placed on the street without any income. His near-retirement age, the highest unemployment rate in almost three decades, and the overall poor demand for his skills made it impossible for him to find another job.

As you can see from this example, employers are often liable for displaced employees, even if they believe employees were fired for poor performance. If employers are the ones to blame, it's only fair if they at least provide some assistance to their departing staff. The best assistance is to help them find a job. If that's not possible, reasonable severance pay would surely be helpful.

One of my clients has an impressive program designed specifically for such employees. Instead of terminating them, my client puts them through a 3-month rotation, asking them to perform various jobs in various departments completely unrelated to what they have been doing before. Each participating department manager then submits a review on the employee and states whether or not this employee would be a good fit in their department. Once a positive review is received, this employer tries to place the employee in that department. Most employees end up with a home. If no home is found, they receive a generous severance package and assistance with finding a new job.

This approach may seem too humanistic to some managers. Other finance-oriented managers will say that they can't afford to spend money on dismissed staff, nor do they have time. After all, we live in a capitalistic society where termination is the way of life. Terminated employees are of no use to us, so why bother with them?

Those believing in this Darwinian approach should consider possible consequences of such actions. Some of them are described in chapter 1 of this book, under the section called "Things That Go Wrong: The Importance of Doing It Right." Keep in mind that people adapt to changes. The Darwinian approach may get the rest of your employee pool or other potential candidates applying to work for you to adapt to your style and turn your most important asset (people) against you.

How Do I Help the Employees?

It's easy to say that employees need help, but it's usually hard to give them the desired assistance due to funding or legal concerns. This section explores several ways you can aid employees.

Help them find a job. This is usually the hardest thing to do. After all, most employees only know of one way to find a job—look for newspaper or online ads and send in resumes. Such efforts can be OK but aren't usually as effective in an economic downturn or if the employee is in a niche job that is in low demand. Most employers can't think of ways to help, but they have several ways of doing so.

1. Call your contacts at other firms and see if anyone has any openings.
2. Help employees build a better resume and coach them through the resume submission and job interviewing process.
3. Send your employee to a local county, state, or nonprofit-owned career assistance center. Believe it or not, there are lots of them around, and they can help by funding the employee's education, helping him or her build a resume, and distributing it to potential employers.

4. Offer to be your employee's reference. It's tough for an employee to state he or she was fired at an interview and get a job afterward. This is where your assistance can help break that roadblock. Tell the new prospective employer the truth. Unless this employee was fired because he or she screwed up, you can make a big difference by disclosing that an employee was let go because he or she wasn't the right fit or because a boss couldn't give the employee what he or she wanted. Admit your mistakes here, if needed. It's important not to lie to the potential employer. You will only hurt your employee and yourself if you do. Do keep in mind, however, that you may be found liable in some countries, including the United States, for giving references on fired employees. See "The Aftermath" section of this book for more information.

5. Send them to a career fair. Lots of career fairs are held throughout many countries.

6. Offer advice on additional things your employee can do to find a job. Tell him or her about 20 to 30 new job sites or opportunities. Help the employee publish his or her resume on every one of those sites.

7. Help your employee cope mentally. It's a stressful process. Provide coaching.

Help them financially. Helping employees financially can be easier than helping them find a job. Here are some things you can do to help:

1. Give them a reasonable severance package. Consider what it will take them to find another job. Although any money you give them would be helpful, it would be appropriate to give them enough to survive for a reasonable period of time. It's important to not overdo oneself and give them too much. After all, employees should be highly encouraged to look for another job, not relax at home while they spend your severance money.

2. Consider paying for their benefits for a reasonable period of time. Unemployed people often drop, or are dropped from, their insurance when they lose their jobs without realizing that the loss of insurance may lead to even bigger financial problems in the long term.

3. Let them have their unemployment checks. Many employers deny employee's benefits by stating that employees have been fired for cause. Sometimes this cause is valid; sometimes it's not. Typically their motivation in denying the unemployment benefits comes from two sources: potential increase in unemployment insurance premiums (which only applies to some states in the United States) and ego. Many employers believe they can punish employees by denying their benefits. In addition, they don't want their insurance premiums to skyrocket because of some screw-up they just had to let go. The truth is, you may only hurt yourself in the long term if you do this. You already punished them by putting them on the street. Now it's your obligation to help them. Remember, it could have been your mistake!

4. Offer them financial advice. Surprisingly, many people live paycheck to paycheck and don't know how to manage their own debt. A simple phone call or advice can sometimes make a big difference.

Consider the following example. I met a man who wanted to build his credit history and applied for his first credit card. He was an uneducated, poorly paid individual with no assets and loads of debt. Due to the high risk of extending him credit, the credit card company offered him a deal—a credit card with a $200 credit limit, a $300 annual fee, and no grace period. This was a terrible deal, but he had no choice and accepted the offer. After all, he wanted to get a credit card. This is where things started to get even worse. The credit card company gave him a credit card and sent him the first bill. This was a $350 bill. It included the annual fee of $300. Because it had a $200 credit limit, he had an automatic $100 overdraft on his account. As a result, the company charged him a $25 overdraft fee. They also made his bill due immediately and charged a $25 overdue fee because he didn't pay it when he just opened the account. This poor individual couldn't afford to pay the entire amount, so he decided to pay just the minimum $25 that was due. He didn't notice that he had a 19% annual percentage rate of interest on his account, and he wasn't educated enough to figure out that it would take him two years to pay off the credit card. He also didn't realize he will be billed another $300 annual fee in 12 months, increasing his overdraft and putting him even deeper in debt. When I met him, he'd been paying off his credit card for a few years. He had a $600 balance and he hadn't used his credit card a single time. Thankfully, his new employer had a program just for him. This employer covered the $600 balance, helped the employee close this predatory credit card, and helped the employee get a new credit card through the bank by depositing $1,000 in the bank under this employee's name. This man became the most dedicated employee in the firm.

There are numerous other examples of poor financial situations displaced employees were put in.

- I met a woman who said she couldn't find another job because her car broke down and she couldn't afford to buy another one. After careful investigation, I found out that she could afford many cars. She just couldn't afford the specific luxury car she wanted. Because she always drove luxury cars, she couldn't even imagine buying a cheaper car. When prompted as to why she didn't purchase a less expensive car, she answered, "Oh! I haven't even thought of that! That's a great idea!"

- I met a woman who was fired from her job and complained that she didn't have enough money to feed her family. Investigation showed that she was in financial trouble because she was spending $150 a week on getting her hair done. Getting her hair done was such a given that she hadn't considered the financial implications of doing so. Her employer offered her $1,000 to pay for food in return for not getting her hair done until she found another job. Although this came as a shock and she found it hard to follow this advice, she took the money and simplified her hairstyle until she found a new job.

- I met a man who had a family of six and no health insurance. He thought his insurance premium was too high ($600 per month) and he couldn't afford it, so he dropped it when he was let go. What he never considered was that he had a sick child who incurred medical bills of $1,000 to $10,000 per month. It made more sense for him to pay $600, but he didn't see it as an option. In fact, he took his health insurance for granted to such an extent that he didn't even know how much the insurance company had been paying for his child every month. In order to help him not fall into this financial trap, his employer prepaid for his insurance for 3 months.

The previous examples clearly indicate that many fired and laid-off employees need financial assistance.

Be innovative. There are many other approaches employers may take to assist employees who are displaced. The possibilities are infinite. The following are some real-world examples that will give you ideas.

- One of my old clients was a Fortune 500 company with almost 100,000 employees around the world. This company has developed a centralized software system for tracking all jobs, projects, resource allocations, and demand for skills around the globe. Originally this system was built in order to allow the company's HR team to manage their recruitment efforts. Eventually, it became the way to optimize the firm's resource allocation. Any time an employee was displaced for any reason other than a screw-up, he or she would be asked to use the software system and search for projects that require his or her expertise. The employee was typically given a few weeks to find something and was allowed to pick any project or job he or she wanted, whether it was short or long term. HR would then submit the employee's candidacy to the hiring manager without disclosing that this employee was removed from the previous job. If no match was found within a few weeks, HR would intervene and try to find a project for this employee, even if this employee wasn't too crazy about it. The employee would get paid a full salary while looking for a project and would only get dismissed if nothing was found within 1 to 2 months.
- I helped one of my clients come up with a highly successful system of "6-month commitments." Every employee was given the list of expectations and was constantly measured against them and provided with very honest feedback. This feedback was near real time, allowing employees to cor-rect their performance immediately. No one was ever fired for poor performance. The firm would always commit to

giving employees at least 6 months' worth of work. At the end of each 6-month period, the company would review the employee's performance for the past half a year and decide whether or not it wanted to renew its employment commitment for another 6 months. Great performers would get new commitments. Poor performers would end up on the street. Every employee understood the system; they had to perform well in order to stay beyond 6 months. Every poor performer was warned about his or her deficient performance far in advance and was told that the commitment may not get renewed. Almost all poor performers would find new jobs by the time the company had to renew its commitments. This was a win-win strategy. The company was able to retain the best staff. Weak performers would be in a financially stable position while looking for another job. They were thankful to the company for learning what they needed to do to improve and for giving them an opportunity to look for another job when this one did not work out. Many of them had never heard candid feedback before and never knew what was wrong with their performance.

• One of my clients terminated several unskilled employees who couldn't perform well in the poor weather conditions they were placed in. These people originally joined the company from their hometowns located in major metropolitan areas and were flown into a distant area far north to perform work. In order to assist them, the company paid for their trip back to their hometowns, gave them a 3-month severance package, and paid to send them to a computer literacy school so they could learn basic computer skills and get better jobs. Due to the company size and the rate at which this type of termination was happening, the firm eventually brought the computer literacy classes in-house. As the company grew bigger, it started sourcing some of the entry-level office labor from its own school. Ironically, displaced workers competed with outside candidates so much that the going joke was that one would first have to travel north and get fired in order to get an office job with the firm.

No matter how much assistance you can provide your terminated employees, remember that most likely they were terminated because they were a bad fit or poorly led in the first place. These employees are not criminals. The fact that you hired them initially shows that you thought of them highly at some point. It's only fair to treat them as human beings. Fair treatment will minimize personal damage to your employees as well as damage to your organization and your brand.[6]

You Are Fired! Surprise!

One should never be as surprised to get fired as the person walking into the room full of balloons with friends screaming, "Surprise! Happy Birthday!" Unfortunately, most firings do carry an element of surprise; in most cases this surprise is better described as shock. This shock causes people to "go postal,"[7] file multimillion-dollar discrimination lawsuits, and tell your existing employees and prospective candidates what your company is *really* about. There are two concepts you should practice as a leader to reduce surprises.

Managers should be candid. People often sugarcoat and filter what they say. Such lack of candor can prove very damaging to an organization. It can happen across the board—budget meetings, status updates, and so on. Most often candor is missing from performance reviews. Sometimes managers lie in order to motivate others, and sometimes they just don't want to offend their employees or create conflict. In some cases it's even a company requirement. People think it's cruel, not nice, unfair, or simply hard to tell employees that they aren't doing a good job. What should sound like "you constantly screw up because you never follow up and always forget to finish your work" is usually translated into "you are doing a terrific job and can do even better if you try to remember things." The challenge is that this translation isn't fair to the employees either. People like to do a good job. They don't like being lied to. They want to know what they can do to improve and where they can go in the future. They want to know how their career will progress. They want to know if they'll have a job tomorrow. It is cruel and unfair to not disclose this information to them! It's even worse to mislead them by sugarcoating their performance appraisal.

I once had to fire a man who spent over a decade with the company. His performance was poor, but his boss didn't want to tell him that. Instead of giving him feedback about things he did wrong, his boss would state that this employee was doing a great job and then go and finish this employee's work himself. At some point, this boss was performing 90% of the work. A decade later, this employee still believed he was doing a terrific job. This employee ended up getting fired. Can you imagine how he felt when he found out his feedback was falsified for the past 10 years? He thought he was building a career. He expected a promotion at some point. Instead, he found out that he wasted 10 years of his life and achieved nothing.

One of my clients had a junior executive who was being groomed for a more senior position. He had spent 4 years running special projects, learned many things, and was ready to take on something bigger. He was under the impression that he was doing a superb job and he was about to get promoted. But promotion wasn't coming his way. This executive never knew that his boss wasn't happy about his performance and had no plans to promote him. When I looked into this situation, I discovered that while the boss's concerns were valid, they could all be easily remediated only if proper feedback had been provided to this executive. This executive was a star with potential far exceeding that of his boss. But his boss didn't let him uncover this potential. Instead of giving this employee feedback and putting him on the path of becoming a more senior person, the boss limited this employee's responsibilities to those the boss thought the employee could do just fine. What looked like 4 years of learning to this employee ended up being 4 years of wasted time. When I had a conversation with the boss about uncovering this employee's potential by giving him feedback, she disagreed with me and stated she didn't believe the employee was capable and therefore any feedback would be pointless.

Examples like the previous one would never happen if managers were candid in the first place. Now think about your own work environment. Here are some questions to ask yourself:

- Do you think you receive honest feedback and performance appraisals from your boss?
- Do you give timely and honest feedback and performance appraisals to your subordinates? If yes, do your subordinates agree that you do?

- Think of the last few times you weren't so candid to your staff
  about their performance. What do you think would be different today if you were more open to them? If you think your
  honesty would deliver negative results, think of ways to make
  them positive.
- Think of a person in your organization you don't like but have
  to work with. Have you expressed your feelings to this person
  so you can work out any issues, or do you put on a fake smile
  and work with the person as if nothing happened?
- How much time do you waste by not being candid? Can you
  become more productive if you open up? For example, if something bothers you in the way your boss does business, what
  have you done to correct this?

People should see it coming. Contrary to what most managers think,
employees are capable of seeing where they stand and that their termination is coming. In a majority of the cases where they don't, it's due to
poor communication between a manager and an employee. Consider the
following two scenarios.

Scenario 1

A manager submitted paperwork to HR asking to terminate an employee.
When asked whether the employee knew about it, the manager said,
"Well, yeah, I told him several times how to do his work but he is doing
it wrong. So he better know he will get fired for this."

Scenario 2

A manager created a project plan outlining his employee's tasks and due
dates. He sat down with the employee and described the end goals, how
they should be achieved, when they should be achieved, and what may
happen to the firm if this project wasn't completed successfully. He further explained to this employee that his performance would be measured
against the end goals and it was up to him to make sure this project
was executed properly in order to insure the success of the firm. This
employee tried to execute the plans but couldn't complete the task on

time, resulting in the loss of the firm's largest customer. As a result, the firm faced a major layoff and reported a net loss. The employee running this project was terminated.

In which of the previous scenarios do you think the person saw it coming? I've seen many cases of Scenario 1 and it's rare to see the employee predict that he or she is getting terminated. Telling employees how to do their job is not the same as telling them they'll get fired if they don't do it properly. Scenario 2 is more straightforward. A large number of people will actually resign before you even approach them about firing.

I had to terminate a senior employee once for missing a critical deadline. Perhaps this was the easiest termination I ever had to do. The conversation with this employee looked approximately like this:

Day 1

> *Matt*: Jack, here's a project for you. It's due in 30 days. This deadline is critical. If we don't deliver, our largest customer will fire us as a vendor. It may cost us a lot of jobs.
> *Jack*: I understand. No problem. I'll get it done.
> *Matt*: Do you think the 30-day timeframe is feasible?
> *Jack*: Absolutely!
> *Matt*: Do you need any help?
> *Jack*: No, piece of cake! I'll do it myself!

Day 20

> *Matt*: Jack, you have 10 days left. Any concerns? Do you need any help?
> *Jack*: Nope! It will get done by the due date. I promise!
> *Matt*: How far are you from being done?
> *Jack*: I am about 80% there. Most of the hard work is done.

Day 25

> *Matt*: Jack, I know you have 5 days left, but I am getting concerned. Will you be done?

Jack: Absolutely! I am on track to get done in exactly 5 days.

Matt: Jack, you realize the importance of this project and how critical this deadline is, right?

Jack: Yep! I know if I don't finish we'll make our largest customer very upset. It'll get done.

Matt: You realize that I can't get an extension in case you are late. Is there something I should know?

Jack: Matt, you shouldn't worry. It will get done. No extension is needed.

Matt: OK, do you want me to assign someone to help you?

Jack: No worry, Matt. It's almost done. I am about 95% there.

Day 30

Matt: Jack, it's due today. How are we doing?

Jack: You will have it by close of business today. It's almost done.

Matt: Jack, you are scaring me. Are you sure you can get it done by 5 pm?

Jack: Absolutely! I will send it to the customer no later than 5 pm. I'll let you know if there's a problem.

Matt: Let me get someone to help you . . .

Jack: No, I am fine. I'll finish it myself. I promise. I've never been late on my deliverable before! I am 99% there and I just need to put some finishing touches in here . . .

Day 31

Matt: Jack, Did you submit the deliverable to the customer yesterday?

Jack: No. I know I promised but I am not done yet. I found a problem.

Matt: You realize that this deliverable was critical, right?

Jack: I know, but I have a problem I have to fix. Sorry, it will be late.

Matt: Jack, you promised!

Jack: I know, but I still have to work on it. You will have it tomorrow.

Day 32

> *Matt*: Jack, are you done?
>
> *Jack*: No, I need another day or so.
>
> *Matt*: Jack, do you realize what situation we are in now?
>
> *Jack*: Yes. I am sorry. I know our customer is upset. I am doing everything I can to finish.
>
> *Matt*: Jack, I asked you several times if you need help and you said you were OK. We are late. We are in trouble. I am speechless now.
>
> *Jack*: I know and I am sorry.

Day 33

> *Matt*: Jack, are you done?
>
> *Jack*: No. I am not.
>
> *Matt*: Jack, this is affecting your performance and the performance of the firm as a whole.
>
> *Jack*: I know. Frankly, I am surprised that you haven't fired me yet.
>
> *Matt*: Hmmm. Do you think you need to be fired?
>
> *Jack*: I've been thinking about it. I totally screwed up. I don't want to get fired but I think I need to be. As a matter of fact, I'd like to resign myself. I would like to give you a 30-day notice. In these 30 days, I would appreciate an opportunity to correct the situation and pass all of my work to another person.

Conversations between a manager and an employee rarely look like this. What was unique about this conversation is the fact that an employee saw the firing coming. He knew his end goals. He knew what would happen if he didn't succeed. He recognized failure when it occurred and knew he was getting fired as a result.

As you can see, effective communications can get you pretty far. If employees know where they stand, they often quit themselves or at least they get ready for the day they get terminated. I've seen countless cases of employees predicting the exact date they will be let go. They always knew the reason. The conversation was always short:

Matt: Jack, let's talk about your performance on Project A.
Jack: I know, I screwed up. I promised but couldn't deliver.
Matt: Do you know what this means?
Jack: Yes, I have to look for another job.

If you can take the conversation to this level, you've achieved your goal. Here are some questions you can ask yourself:

- Do I see any flaws or opportunities for improvement in my staff members? If yes, have I communicated them?
- Do my people understand what's expected of them?
- Do my people know the end goals? Do they see my vision? Do they understand and agree with the mission? Are they aware of rewards and punishments?
- If someone were to approach my poor performers today and ask them how they think they are doing, what would they say? Would they agree with your view?

Help Employees Understand

One of the common mistakes managers make is they assume that employees understand why they are being fired. Of course, if you follow the practice of candor described earlier and employees see it coming, you won't have to communicate the why. But people aren't perfect. You may still have people who don't understand. Or maybe you have legacy employees with whom you haven't communicated because you hadn't read this book yet. The point is, sometimes you have to explain the reasons to them when you let them go.

Some managers terminate employees without any explanations. The best explanation employees sometimes get is that their services are no longer needed. Of course, there are legal concerns here. After all, the more you tell them, the more you may be liable (see the next section of this chapter). But there are also several reasons you want to explain the termination to employees. Many of them are listed in an earlier section of this book titled "Things That Go Wrong: The Importance of Doing It Right." In addition, it's only humane and fair to tell your employees what they did wrong so they don't repeat their mistakes again.

One of the worst ways to point out an employee's performance issue is to blame him for what he has done, criticize him, and point at the facts, unless you are talking to an executive who is used to the culture of candor and has been trained on, and appreciates, direct communications. It's only a normal human reaction to self-defend against any attack. Even if the employee you are criticizing agrees with the facts and understands the consequences of what he has done, he will defend himself if you approach him with direct criticism. Take a look at the next two examples. Which one looks more effective to you?

The first example approaches the employee with direct criticism, hoping that the employee will understand and apologize for what was

Table 2.1. Examples of ineffective and effective conversations

Example 1	Example 2
Manager: Jack, you really screwed up! You were supposed to complete the project by Friday and you aren't even close!	*Manager*: Jack, would you mind shedding some light into why the project wasn't completed by Friday?
Employee: Of course! I had five other priorities. I didn't get a chance to finish this project yet.	*Employee*: Yeah, I had other priorities.
Manager: But I told you it was due on Friday! If you didn't have time, why didn't you stay after work to finish it?	*Manager*: I appreciate that. Let me ask you—how do you think our client feels about the fact that you didn't finish the project?
Employee: Because I promised my wife I'd take her to dinner.	*Employee*: Probably upset about it . . .
Manager: Dinner?! You'd rather take your wife to dinner than do your job?	*Manager*: What can you do in the future to make sure our customer isn't upset with us?
Employee: Are you saying I am not doing my job? I've been busting by butt for you . . .	*Employee*: I guess I could have stayed after work to finish it. I promised my wife to take her to dinner, but I guess I could have rescheduled that.

done. While this works with some people, the second example is much more effective with the great majority of them. This conversation is centered around questions, rather than statements. There is no criticism. A set of questions triggers the employee to think and come up with answers him or herself, making it sound like the answers were his or her own ideas and making the person feel important. Note several key phrases in these examples: "I appreciate that!" and "What can you do in the future?" These phrases are magic! The first one keeps the conversation positive. The second one prompts the employee to come up with the solution without pointing out directly what he was supposed to do. There's another magic phrase—"Bless your heart!" You can say anything you want to an employee, follow with this magic phrase, and be taken positively:

John, you just haven't put enough hours into the project, bless your heart!

or

Steve, you've been lying to me all this time. You are an idiot, bless your heart!

Try this approach and see magic at work. People can take anything from you if you follow your feedback with this phrase!

If feedback isn't delivered to employees properly, the feedback time is wasted. Consider the following termination example. My client had an employee whose performance was poor. He was a nice guy, but he was in the wrong job. My client had numerous conversations with him indicating that his performance required improvement. He was told exactly what he was lacking and what he needed to do to improve. Every time my client and this employee had such conversations, this poor performer agreed with the assessment and promised to take specific actions to get better. But he never tried. My client gave him feedback, both verbal and written. This employee signed his own performance evaluation as well as personnel action form indicating the type of actions he needs to perform in order to improve his performance. His boss followed up on every task this employee was supposed to do and tried everything possible to make sure this employee executed their tasks. Nothing worked. Before my client let this employee go, he had another executive, whom this employee considered a great friend, have a frank conversation with him. The president of the company, another great friend who brought him into the firm in the first place, talked to him as well. Every conversation with this employee confirmed that he understood and he was going to do something about his performance. Unfortunately, nothing worked. When all of these efforts failed, my client decided to terminate him. When my client brought the poor performer into his office and explained why he was there, he was shocked. The numerous conversations they had before were worthless. This employee behaved as if there was never a single conversation about his performance before. I asked my client how feedback was given to this employee. The answer was that it always sounded approximately like this:

Manager: Jack, you've been assigned a task to assist Robert, but you failed to deliver.

Jack: Really? I thought I did everything Robert wanted me to do that I knew how to do.

Manager: That's not good enough. If you don't know how to do something, you have to figure it out or tell me that you need help. Will you do that for me next time?

Jack: OK, no problem.

Conversations like this may look straightforward. After all, this employee confirmed that he will behave differently next time. However, he never confirmed that he understood the problem his manager was trying to solve. I sat down with this employee and took a different approach. It went approximately like this:

Matt: Jack, I've heard about the task you had to do for Robert . . .

Jack: Yeah, can you believe it? My manager never told me how to perform this task and he expected me to perform! And then he had the guts to tell me that it wasn't good enough and he expected me to do better next time! How am I supposed to do it if I don't have the skills required?

Matt: Jack, suppose you walk into McDonald's and order a cheeseburger. The cashier takes your money but doesn't give you a cheeseburger and doesn't explain why. When you ask him what happened to your food, he responds that he doesn't know how to prepare it and it's not even his job. How would you feel about this?

Jack: God, I would probably yell at this idiot! It's his job to know. If he doesn't know, he should go and ask someone else, perhaps his manager. When I go to McDonald's, I expect them to know how to make my food.

Matt: Great! Let's go back to the task you were trying to accomplish for Robert and see how your McDonald's strategy would apply here. Robert thinks that your department is McDonald's. He sends a request and expects it to be completed. This request is a cheeseburger. You are the cashier at McDonald's. You don't know how to make Robert's cheeseburger. You just mentioned that you have some advice for the cashier . . .

Jack: Yeah, I said he can ask someone else, such as his manager.

Matt: That's a great idea! Can you apply this advice in your case?

Jack: Of course I can!

Matt: Now, let's go back to Robert. How do you think he felt when you didn't deliver what he wanted?

Jack: He was probably as frustrated as I'd be if my cheeseburger wasn't given to me at McDonald's.

There are two key components that made this conversation different. First, the problem was presented—it indicated that Robert expected results and they were never delivered. Second, the solution wasn't shoved down this employee's throat. Instead, a set of questions was asked prompting this employee to understand the problem and make his own decision about how this problem can be fixed. Of course, the manager has to stay in control while using this questioning technique and make sure the employee stays on the right track. Questions can be adjusted to give the employee a suggestion that he would take as his own idea.

Matt: What do you think you can do differently in the future in order to avoid the problem?

Jack: Oh, I don't know. Probably nothing.

Matt: Well, what do you think about asking John or Frank for help?

Jack: Hmmm. Let me think . . . Frank is definitely an expert in this field. But Bob knows even more. I'll ask Bob.

Note the verbiage picked by the manager. Instead of saying, "You should ask John or Frank," the manager said, "What do you think about asking John or Frank." Although it seems like a regular statement to a manager, the first one may prompt a negative reaction, such as "John doesn't know how to do this" or "They are too busy." The second one, however, makes the person think about it and show his expertise by making his own decision. There are other phrases a manager can use to force his employee think in that direction:

Who do you think you can consult to solve this problem?

or

I know you don't trust Frank. Are there other people you trust that can help?

or

I've seen people in the past solve this problem by consulting Bob. Can you do the same?

Sentences like these can change the employee's train of thought, moving him from the defensive to problem-solving mode.

If executed properly, the questioning technique can turn into an effective feedback tool. This technique can also be used to help people understand why they are being fired.

Legal Issues

This is not a law book and laws differ from state to state and from country to country, so it's hard to describe all legal considerations in one section of this book. But one should definitely consider how, why, and for what reasons one terminates employees to see if there are any legal consequences. Some terminations are hard from the legal perspective because they can cause lawsuits. World-famous Willie Gary won over 150 multi-million-dollar lawsuits against giants like Wal-Mart proving they were discriminating while terminating some of their employees. I personally witnessed a racial discrimination lawsuit filed by an employee who was fired for "being incompetent." This employee did happen to be incompetent in that particular job, but she won the lawsuit. Her next employer was thinking about terminating her for the same exact reason but decided to wait until she chose to leave rather than risk legal action.

Here are some other examples I've witnessed that are shocking:

- A large employer laid off a small percentage of its sales force that was performing worse than average. Coincidentally, people in this round of layoffs shared a similar demographic—they were all over the age of 50. This employer got sued for age discrimination and ended up settling with employees he terminated for a large amount of money.
- An employer refused to terminate a poor performer because he was the only minority staff member in the team of 20 people.
- An employee filed a "wrongful termination" lawsuit against his employer. After his employer presented evidence in court clearly showing that termination was for cause, this employee appealed to the judge with a statement that it was simply wrong to fire a person and put him on the street without money. He won the lawsuit and collected money from his previous employer.
- An employee filed a lawsuit against her employer for racial discrimination. She stated in court that she did a great job and therefore the firm had no reason to fire her other than the fact that she was a minority. The firm couldn't prove that she

was doing a bad job and never documented the reason for the firing. The employee won the lawsuit.

While some cases of discrimination are legitimate, others are clever products of the world's top legal professionals. In order to prevent these lawsuits from happening, managers can follow a simple principle consisting of the following concepts:

Say less. The more you talk, the more you will wish you didn't say when you are taken to court. Every word out of your mouth is an opportunity for someone to question.

Be fair. U.S. law requires equal treatment of employees, especially the ones working in the same position. If you offer severance to one employee but not the other, you may end up in court.

Question your own actions. For every action you perform, think whether someone may find it to be discriminating. I've seen a racial discrimination lawsuit arise from a psychological profile of a prospective candidate. After he was denied the job, he claimed that the test he was given allowed the employer to find out his race based on his answers. Although this employer made a case that this test had been developed by Harvard PhDs and used by thousands of employers to predict future performance, the judge ruled in favor of the employee.

Prevent further contact. Every time you or your employees contact the person who was terminated, you risk disclosing information that needs to stay private. I once had to terminate an employee for making a major screw-up, resulting in a critical security breach. Although I disclosed the reason for the termination to the rest of the staff, one of my employees called the fired employee and told him there was a rumor going on that this wasn't a termination for cause but rather a termination because he had said the wrong thing to the wrong people. The fired employee got upset and sued the employer for badmouthing him. I've seen another case where an employee called a terminated staffer and told him that he was terminated because of the firm's financial trouble and not for cause. This staffer then sued the employer, claiming that this was a layoff, demanding severance and punitive damages to clean his name. He further stated that he couldn't get another job because he had to disclose to prospective employers that he was fired from his last position. His employer ended up paying his salary while this employee was looking for another job.

Dignity

Many terminations I've witnessed followed a similar pattern. The boss would get upset with his or her employee's performance. The boss would put his or her mind in the "I'll punish you" state, call the employee into the office, and tell the employee everything he or she thinks. After all, it's a punishment. This conversation can contain everything from pure frank talk to screaming. It usually starts as a monologue, with the employer spitting out everything on his or her mind. It then turns into an argument, with the employee defending against the onslaught and the employer having fun arguing, knowing he or she has the power to terminate the employee. Both parties believe they are right in the argument. At the end of the day, the employer feels happy or relieved terminating an employee, thinking it was the right thing and he or she did a good job punishing the evildoer. The employee thinks he was right and he will figure out how to punish the boss, who turned out to be a total jerk.

Terminations like this are awful from many standpoints. One of them is the fact that this employee lost dignity. Some managers believe that there's nothing wrong with that, but there are three main reasons dignity should be preserved.

Corporate culture. No matter how much you hide it, your employees will see what you did. While many managers believe that it's a great way to teach employees what may happen to them if they disobey, the reality is that most employees will actually get upset with such treatment. Their morale will go down and performance will degrade.

My father witnessed a case in which the boss decided to terminate this employee in front of the other staff members. This manager screamed at his employee and terminated him in front of his colleagues. This employee then punched his boss in front of 30 speechless witnesses and left. The boss ended up in the emergency room. When he recovered, he filed charges against the employee. To his surprise, not a single witness confirmed that they had seen the fight. Some of the witnesses even went out of their way to tell the police that the boss was famous for making up stories.

In this particular case, the company culture had been destroyed. Many employees had left; others still worked there and hated their boss. Their productivity level went down to ridiculous levels. So did their willingness to do something for their boss and their company or perform work in general.

Although most terminations don't end up in physical fights, employee morale gets destroyed with terminations like this all the time.

Humanistic. We are all human beings and we like being treated with respect. That's a basic need derived from our social values. When you "punish" a person by terminating him or her, you already make a statement. What more do you need to say? There is no reason to hurt or belittle a person. It's tough enough to lose a job. Stay humane and don't hurt him or her anymore.

It's your mistake. Recall the reasons people don't work out in their jobs, as we've discussed in the "Misfits, Poor Fits, and Screw-Ups" section of this chapter. Often people don't work out because they were a bad fit or because of poor leadership. Bad fit can be linked to leadership as well. It is a leader's responsibility to put the right people in the right jobs. If an employee fails, it's the leader's fault for putting the employee there in the first place. So if it's your fault for placing the wrong person on the job or for leading improperly, why "punish" him or her? Show some respect and let the employee leave with dignity!

As you can see, preserving dignity is important, even though doing so may be tricky at times, especially if you have negative feelings toward the employee you are letting go.

So how do you preserve employee's dignity? Here are some tricks.

Pretend that this was the best employee that has ever worked for you. Think about ways you'd part with your best employee. Would you thank him or her for their efforts (even if the outcome is not what you would have liked)? Would you take him or her to lunch? Would you wish the employee luck? Think of positive emotions. After all, it may not be the employee's fault that he or she is being let go.

You may think that it's ridiculous to thank the employee for their effort even if it didn't work out and take him or her to lunch. But think outside the box. Did this employee do anything good at all or was he or she a 100% waste of your time? If this employee was a complete waste of time, was the employee in the right job? Did he or she at least attempt to do the work you assigned? If they are able to confront reality, a lot of employers find that they can give a lot of credit to terminated employees. If that's the case, there's nothing wrong with thanking them. You may not necessarily thank them for a good job, but you may at least thank them for the time they've given your firm or for attempting to do a good job.

You may also point out some things they did really well. Taking them to lunch is purely your choice, but it may be a good way to have a conversation about how you can help them find the next job. Be careful with what you say at this lunch though, especially if you drink alcohol.

Have a decent conversation with your employee. Firing people is the hardest job. You have an urge to keep this conversation to a minimum, but you owe it to your employee to have a conversation that shows respect. Your employee may have lots of questions. Ignoring him or her and cutting it short may look disrespectful. Whenever possible, this conversation should be between an employee and immediate supervisor, not an HR representative or some other third party, although it may be necessary for them to be present. This dialogue should be private. The fewer people who are exposed to it, the better. It should also be direct. There should be no sweet talking or schmoozing. There's no point in asking your employee how his or her day was or how his or her spouse is doing. Talk to them in person, not over the phone or over email.

Carefully prepare for this conversation. You have to go in the room with a clear head. If you have any negative feelings toward this employee, reschedule the termination. You have to be objective and have neutral feelings toward the person.

Words mean a lot to people at this point. Choose them carefully. Don't use words that hurt people, such as "you are fired" or "you screwed up." Pick words that reflect the truth in the most politically correct way. Table 2.2 lists some examples.

Let your employee leave unnoticed. Some employers make a show out of walking their terminated employees out so they can teach the rest of

Table 2.2. Word Alternatives

Bad words	Good alternative
You are fired.	We have to part ways.
You screwed up.	Your performance hasn't been as effective as desired.
I told you many times . . .	As I am sure you can remember, we've discussed this matter on more than one occasion.
You lied to me.	You haven't been entirely truthful in your conversations with me.

their staff a lesson. While teaching your staff a lesson may be good, it is disrespectful to the employee to do it at this point. You will have plenty of opportunities to do it later (see "The Aftermath" section later in this chapter). Try to do everything possible to have this employee pack and leave the building unnoticed. If you have to have a security escort, try to make them invisible. The escort can walk with this employee but not look like he or she is escorting the employee. Don't tell other employees about the termination until after this employee leaves.

One of my clients came up with a very polite way to escort employees out. Of course, this method can have some side effects. Some employees may not be too happy having other people handle their personal belongings. An HR representative calls the employee to be terminated into the conference room located right next to the front door of the building. While they are having a conversation, a member of the security team will walk into the employee's workspace and pack his or her belongings. If the employee has a personal office, the door will get closed, so no one can see the packing process. The packing process is always very quick and discreet. Usually the security officer will visit the employee's work space after hours the day before the employee termination to assess the level of effort required to pack. Once items are packed, they are taken in sealed boxes outside. The terminated employee is quickly walked out of the building. This is possible due to the conference room's proximity to the front door.

This strategy isn't perfect but it's the one they have to follow due to very stringent security requirements. One mistake may cost this client millions of dollars.

Give your employee some reasonable freedom. Some employees choose not to stay unnoticed or want to pack their own stuff. Unless they are disruptive or your security requirements call for an alternative process, let them have some freedom. I've seen numerous cases of employees walking around and saying good-bye or wishing good luck to others. I've seen others who wanted to pack their own stuff. I've had an employee who had a lot of personal files on his work computer and he wanted to copy them onto a CD. Unless it is a security issue, whether it's saying good-bye or copying files, let them do it. Just be careful if you think they are disgruntled. They may end up telling every employee what a jerk their boss is or how bad this company had been.

Preserving Values

Every company has values. They can range from quality to work environment. Whatever they are, they matter a lot to people in your organization. Whenever you make a decision to let people go, you have to see how your decision and the way you do it is aligned with those values.

The first thing you have to do is determine what those values are. There are some that are defined by top leadership, such as product quality or commitment to getting things done on time. There are others that are perceived by employees, such as respect, recognition, and ability to grow within the firm. These perceived values aren't easily visible or recognized by managers, but they do exist and they do matter a lot. The easiest way to find them is to perform a company-wide survey with an open-ended question such as "What do you like about your job and/or this company?" Surveys like this can uncover hidden truths about the firm. For example, one such survey I performed for a client showed that people greatly valued the fact that they had flexible work hours. One day the firm had asked a group of its employees to forgo the flexibility and work a set schedule. Some people agreed, while others refused. When this client decided to terminate an employee for not wanting to work a set schedule after he had been with the firm for 5 years, this sent the wrong message to the rest of the group. In order to prevent employees from believing their most favorite benefit was now gone, the client went out to the rest of the team and promoted the goal of getting final results accomplished regardless of schedules. These goals were so challenging that employees always had to work extra hours, forcing employees to be present at work during core hours the employer wanted them there. This organizational change took a long time to completely get embedded in the culture, but it had a great effect. Some people now believed they have flexible schedules as long as they get their work done. As a result, employees are no longer terminated for having unfavorable schedules. Instead, the company terminates them for being unable to deliver results. Of course there's a side effect, too. Most employees' job satisfaction fell due to their employer's actions. Some employees left. Others saw a degradation of performance.

Here's a great exercise you can use to see how well your termination process is aligned with your values. List all known company values and perform a survey asking staff what they think their company or their personal values are. Then think about each and every step of your termination process, including things you do or things you say. For every step in the process, see how it impacts any of the values you listed. Any time you find an action that may negatively impact your values, see how you can fix it. Be honest with yourself when you conduct this exercise. Being able to confront reality is key to execution here.

In a perfect world, an exercise like this should produce no results. In the real world, it often does. At the end of the day, an exercise like this will help you preserve the corporate culture and prevent employees from being disgruntled.

Making the Move

If you follow the general advice of this book and provide constant, timely, candid feedback, deliver it in a proper way, and show great signs of leadership, terminating people will be much easier. In fact, you can get people to quit on their own.

Having People Quit on Their Own

I've seen numerous cases where employees resigned voluntarily after seeing that they just can't deliver. Some did it out of fear that they would get terminated. Others did it because they thought it was the right thing to do. A lot of people, however, wait to get terminated, hoping it will never happen. When confronted with termination, many choose to quit themselves.

This may or may not be a good idea, depending on local laws. Some states won't give people unemployment benefits if they quit themselves. Other states require severance to be paid to terminated employees, regardless of the termination reason, making it unattractive for employees to quit.

Employers should carefully consider local laws and, if legally and financially feasible, give employees a way to resign voluntarily. This is a very humanistic approach. After all, there's a good chance this employee is getting terminated for being in the wrong job or for having a less than effective manager. But you should be careful with such offers as well. I've seen cases where employees used an option to voluntarily quit to sue employers. They would state that they signed the resignation letter under duress or that they would get fired if they didn't sign it. Once they turned their voluntary resignation into a forceful termination, they sued for severance or unemployment benefits and claimed gender or age discrimination. Some states even consider voluntary quitting as termination if employees are put in the position where they don't have any choice but to quit. Some will even consider it wrongful termination.

Because this approach can have legal consequences, employers are urged to consult their labor attorneys before implementing a process of allowing employees to resign voluntarily.

Write-Ups

Almost every firm has some kind of a system that documents employee performance, coaching, or any sort of feedback. While documentation serves as a good tool from the legal standpoint, one should consider its effectiveness in changing employee performance.

I've seen numerous cases where employers created write-ups, stating that the employee will get terminated after a reasonable timeframe (usually 30 days) if he or she doesn't change certain things about performance. I've asked many employers to tell me how often such write-ups turned employees around and found such turnarounds to be rare. Whenever it did happen, I questioned how this write-up was different from any coaching given to the employee prior to this one. In most cases, this was the first time the employee was told about his or her performance. In 100% of the cases, previous coaching was simply ineffective.

I am not suggesting that write-ups are ineffective. Well-written write-ups can go a long way. But I do suggest that write-ups shouldn't be used as a tool to change an employee's performance at the time of termination. I also suggest that write-ups should serve as a secondary tool. The first one should be a very effective one-on-one conversation.

In fact, a simple conversation may open people's minds. Employees don't perform poorly because they feel like it or because they are evil. There's usually a good explanation behind employee's behavior. Getting to that explanation requires a skill that's obvious but hard to master: listening. I've conducted countless employee-coaching sessions for my clients and found an easy-to-recognize pattern most managers fail to see.

Consider the following conversation:

Manager: Jack, I have a serious problem with your performance. I've asked you to produce 50 widgets but you've
only produced 45. Here's a write-up. If you don't start
producing 50 widgets a day in the next week, you will be
let go. Please sign here.

Employee: What do you mean? I wasn't able to produce 50
because my equipment was broken. That's not my fault! I am
not signing anything!

Manager: Jack, if you had a problem with the machinery, you
should have told me. You failed to do that. Please sign here. I
expect you to produce 50 widgets a day.

Employee: That's ridiculous. You know it wasn't my fault!

This conversation will probably last for a considerable period of time
with no results. At the end of this conversation, the manager will feel
confident that the employee understood the performance issue. The
employee will feel horrible because he or she got blamed for something
that wasn't his or her fault. The employee will feel dissatisfied with the
boss, the conversation, and his future with the firm. He will get annoyed,
frustrated, demotivated, and possibly unwilling to continue work or be
loyal to the firm. Most managers don't see it this way. They believe that
their employees are smart enough to understand the issue. But employees are humans. They have their own beliefs, concerns, or understanding of each issue. Consider what would happen if you tried to use this
technique to convince a religious person that there's no God. Writing up
and forcing your point of view down the employee's throat won't get you
far. You may think the two things are different. But here's a trick: views
are views, beliefs are beliefs. People believe in God, their political party,
and many other things. They also believe they are right when you have a
performance-related conversation with them.

So how do you convince them? The answer is simple—don't blame
them for anything, ask a lot of questions, and listen. Let's see how the
conversation above would have been different with such a technique.

Manager: Jack, the plan was to produce 50 widgets, but you've only produced 45. Can you give me some insight into why this happened?

Employee: Yes, my equipment was broken. It took George over a day to fix it.

Manager: Oh, why did it take him so long?

Employee: I don't know. I didn't ask. I just waited until he showed up.

Manager: Well, we planned to produce 50 widgets but we failed to deliver because the machine was down. Going back, what could you have done differently, knowing that you may not be able to deliver all 50 in time because the machine wasn't fixed?

Employee: Hmm. I guess I could have called George and told him it's an emergency and see if he could fix it sooner.

Manager: Great. What would you do if he couldn't do it sooner?

Employee: I could call his supervisor and see if he can speed up the process. I could also call you and see if you can help me.

Manager: This is great. What can you do if no one is available and your equipment can't be fixed in a timely fashion?

Employee: I guess I could make these parts manually.

Manager: What a great idea!

As you can see, the second conversation was more effective than the first. What was different about it?

First, there was no blame. The first version of the conversation had very strong language that implied or assumed that it was the employee's fault. The second version didn't make any assumptions, but rather asked for clarification.

Second, the manager didn't make a single statement, but rather asked questions. Each question was asked in a positive way and provoked some thoughts from the employee. Phrases like "what could you have done differently" reinforce this approach.

Third, the manager listened. He showed that he listened by saying, "Oh" in the beginning of the sentence and by asking questions that followed statements made by the employee.

Finally, the manager controlled the situation. He asked questions that provoked the employee to say exactly what the manager wanted him to say. If the manager didn't like the response (e.g., "I don't know," "I didn't ask"), he followed up with a question that would change the response (e.g., "What could you have done differently?"). If the manager liked the response, he followed up with positive phrases (e.g., "This is great!" "What a great idea!"). Note that these positive phrases don't make a statement but rather reinforce what the employee has said, showing the employee that he is right in his assessment.

As you can see, conversations can be effective if conducted properly.

Now that you know how employees feel when their performance is discussed, think about the way you conduct write-ups. Write-ups don't have conversations. They don't ask questions. They have statements of blame. Human nature dictates that people will defend any allegations. You've already seen examples. Statements of blame won't get you far, especially if your employee won't have a chance to respond.

Because of this, a write-up is *usually* no more than a legal tool designed to protect the employer in case of future legal action. From the legal standpoint, it should absolutely be done. But write-ups won't typically fix any performance issues. Here's something to think about: If you do a write-up and it changes your employee's performance, how effective was the prior coaching you provided to this employee? How will this write-up be different from the ones you've done before or from regular conversations you've had with your employee?

Having the Firing Conversation

Before we discuss what to say, let's talk about communication in general. This final conversation you will have with your employee is a type of communication. Communication isn't just about words. It's also about delivery. It's very important to *communicate* the last message, not just say it.

Here are some things you should do when you have the final conversation:

Try to keep it short. The longer you talk, the harder you make it for the employee to listen and the harder you make it for yourself. Also, the longer you talk, the more you will say that you will later regret saying. This may cause harm from the legal standpoint.

Keep good eye contact. Eye contact shows respect and leadership. Sure, it's very hard to deliver bad news, but you should do it to preserve your employee's dignity and your own face. After all, you are a leader. If a manager can't look his employee in the eyes when terminating the employee, it's usually for one of the two reasons—either the manager has poor leadership skills or the manager hasn't been candid with the employee in the past. Of course, global cultures vary and expectations around eye contact vary as well. You should be sensitive to cultural differences on this issue.

Show confidence. The more confident you look, the less your employee will argue with you. Confidence can be shown in several ways. You must have a firm, decisive voice. It can't vibrate and sound quieter than usual. Don't put any physical items in your hands. Believe it or not, holding a pen will make you feel better, but it may annoy your employee. Sit straight. Don't lie comfortably in an arm chair. You shouldn't look any more comfortable than your employee. Looking more comfortable may send a sign of disrespect. Try to control how quickly you blink your eyes. Speedy blinking is usually a sign of worry. Slow blinking is a sign of confidence.

Bring the appropriate personnel. Don't bring 10 people into the room. The fewer people you have there, the better. However, don't just limit the attendance to yourself. It's usually a good idea if at least one more person, such as a member of the HR team, is there with you. This person can act as your witness in case of a false legal action against you. He can also take notes and give you feedback on things you've done well or things you've done wrong.

Pick the right time. Studies show that employees can cope better if they are let go on a late Friday afternoon. This gives them a weekend to relax and think about it. However, there have been numerous studies done that show that the opposite can be true as well. It's hard to pick the perfect date and time, but here are some pointers:

- Don't let people go right before the holiday. They are usually in a good holiday mood. Don't spoil it for them. While they may deserve to be fired, it shouldn't be up to the employer to also spoil their personal life.
- If you decide to fire them for a screw-up and they are in the middle of fixing this screw-up, consider waiting until they are done. This sends a message to the rest of your team that things must be done and done correctly, no matter what. It also shows

them that you are in control—you can punish employees any time you want, not just immediately after the screw-up. It keeps your employees energized. If an employee screwed up and wasn't immediately terminated, and he or she knows he won't get terminated afterward, the employee will be more likely to relax, lose energy, forget the problem, and screw up again. If the employee knows he or she can get fired any time after the screw up, the adrenaline rush will ensure things will get done afterward.

- Don't do it over the weekend, on a vacation or sick day, or in the evening when the employee has left for the day. Some managers find it easier to fire over the phone or even via email. This is disrespectful. Employees want to see you in person, look you in the eyes, and know that you are truthful with them. They also want to do it during work hours. Don't spoil their vacation or their evening for them.

Pick the right place. The right place isn't necessarily the conference room or an office. I've seen near perfect terminations performed in the airport and a restaurant. You have to play it by ear and see what makes sense. But whatever you do, make sure both you and your employee are comfortable with the place. Taking your employee to a strip club or a baseball game isn't appropriate.

Select the right good-bye package. Usually, the more you can offer your terminated employee, the better. Companies offer anything from severance pay to free health insurance. However, following the strategy of "less is more," there are some benefits employees would rather not get. For example, I've heard of an employer whose policy it was to give all fired employees $20 to go buy themselves a good-bye lunch. While it may be a good gesture from the employer's perspective, employees tend to take benefits like this negatively. Some will feel that their employer was selling them for $20. Others will have millions of things to think about other than a free lunch. And then, of course, why $20? Why not $10 or $50 or $1,000? This number may signify something to your employee. It will make a statement. But remember, the less you say, the better!

Watch your gestures. You should behave the way you normally do with an employee. If your style is to always be friendly, continue being friendly. Dress the same way. If you've never worn a tie in your life, you will freak your employee out if you wear one when you need to terminate him. Don't put hands in your pockets. Make them visible. Speak the way you normally do.

There are many other nonverbal communication mechanisms you should consider. For example, looking at a clock while having a termination conversation may look rude, since it will look like you are trying to get out of there before you answer all of your employee's questions. Writing while you are talking may look bad, too. You should carefully consider whether smiling is good idea. It may be accepted in one of the two ways: either you are laughing at your employee's misfortune, or you are there to wish him luck.

Think about every detail of your delivery and see how it can impact what you are trying to do.

I heard about a funny case from a senior executive while writing this book. This executive had to have a termination conversation with an employee. She had a gut feeling that this employee could cause her physical harm. When she went into the meeting, she brought a stack of papers and a large, heavy paperweight with her. This stack of papers had nothing to do with the meeting, but it was an excuse to have the paperweight there. The purpose of the paperweight was to serve as a defense weapon in case the employee attacked. This manager positioned her hand next to the paperweight such that she could pick it up and hit the employee in less than a second. Thankfully, she didn't need to use it, but having it there made her feel better. When she told me this story, I laughed. She then proceeded to tell me how she came up with the idea. It turned out that her previous boss was once attacked by a disgruntled employee during such termination. The boss was holding a phone in his hand, which he was about to use to make a phone call. To defend himself, he hit the employee in the head with the phone. The employee was knocked out and taken to the emergency room. Ironically, both people kept their jobs. From that point on, this boss would pick up the phone any time any employee would come into his office. This was his defense mechanism at work. He never knew when someone else would attack him.

Although the executive I just referred to had a valid safety concern, bringing defense weapons into a meeting like this could potentially cause legal action. If you know why your boss always holds the phone or the paperweight when you walk in, it will probably make you feel uncomfortable to see your boss. A better way would be to make other security arrangements, such as to have a member of the security staff present, or even a police officer. There are many security companies out there that could help you manage this process.

Now that you know the generalities about how to structure your conversation, you need to actually have it. There may be two types of conversations you will have with your employees. One kind is with people who know where they stand. The other one is with people who don't.

First, let's look at a conversation with people who know where they stand. Both you and your employees are well prepared. In fact, your employees know it may happen any time. It's not a surprise. They already mentally coped with it, potentially started looking for another job, and know enough about you and their performance to predict how this conversation will go.

Although firing is hard to do, this conversation should be fairly easy, since both parties already know what to expect. In a perfect world, you don't even have to say anything. I've seen employees walk in the room and say the words, "So I guess this is it." But oftentimes you still have to say something. There are many ways to deliver the speech, depending on the circumstances. Here's a sample speech that is short, effective, and to the point:

> Jane, I brought you in to discuss a difficult matter. As you know, we are not happy with your performance. We feel you can do better elsewhere. Today we will part company and wish you good luck.[8]

Note the selection of words in this speech. First you start by emphasizing that it's a difficult matter. Then you state the actual problem—you are not happy with your employee's performance. Note that the sentence starts with "as you know," highlighting that this shouldn't be new to the employee. When you make a statement about performance, it's firm and decisive. You shouldn't use phrases that make you look indecisive, such as "I think." It simply states that you aren't happy. Then you state that the employee can do better elsewhere. There's a lot of meaning in one sentence. First, you show your decisiveness by using a very strong word "feel" rather than "believe" or "think." Second, you assure the employee that she is not a total loser and can do better. Third, the word "elsewhere" implies that she is in the wrong job. You are not blaming the employee, but rather suggesting that there's a better fit out there for her. You end the speech by telling the employee she is being let go. Note the selection of words in this sentence. The word "today" is strong and is usually interpreted as "now." It's decisive and shows the employee that there's no way out. Then you say you will part company. It's a nice way to say the employee is being fired without using the ugly "fired" word. By saying "We will" instead of "I'd like to" or "I think I'd like" or "It would be best," you are showing that the decision has been made, you are sure about it, and it won't be debated. You end your monologue by wishing your employee good luck.

Speeches like this should definitely include keywords discussed above. But they should also avoid many keywords. For example, don't apologize! Saying "I am sorry" sends a message of indecisiveness or fault on the part of the employer. If you are truly sorry, you should reconsider this termination. Don't say anything in future tense. Don't add any meaningless words that make the conversation longer. Consider the following sentences: "First, let me thank you for coming here on such a short notice. I know you are busy, but we need to talk . . ."

Although this statement can be read in less than 2 seconds, it's too long and carries very little meaning. You don't have to say "first" or "let me" or "such a short notice." You don't need the second sentence at all, as it simply repeats what you said in the first one. Plus, being busy doesn't matter when you terminate an employee. Saying "we need to talk" is useless. You are already there to talk. You can simply say, "Thank you for coming here."

Of course, each conversation should be tailored toward the reason for termination and any circumstances surrounding the situation. I had a client that needed to terminate a senior technology executive for poor performance. This executive had selected the wrong execution strategy that failed to deliver results as expected. He hadn't accepted his failure, nor did he see the source of his problems. He believed in his strategy and wanted to continue on the old path. The CEO had spoken to him but had failed to convince this executive to switch his tactic. We designed the final conversation with this executive as follows:

> Jack, as you remember, we spoke last week about your choice of strategy for project A. This project failed to deliver, so we needed to change our strategy. You mentioned to me last week that you disagree with my assessment, suggesting that your strategy will still work in the long term. We are now going in a direction other than the one we've been preaching, contradicting our values and the way our firm has worked so far. You have great ideas and you should continue implementing them, but in a company whose vision and values are aligned with yours. I have arranged for you to interview with company Z; they are looking for a person with your skills. I've also arranged with Human Resources to pay you a 3-month salary and cover your health benefits for the next 6 months. Jane will be taking over for you. I'd appreciate a smooth transition. Good luck!

This speech won't work in every case. It was targeted at a specific type of employee. First, this employee was extremely intelligent. He knew that his strategy didn't agree with that of the CEO and that continuing with the strategy would hurt the company. He was a risk taker and was willing to take the risk, hoping his decisions were right and he would succeed as a result. Second, he knew that the CEO felt that his strategy had been a failure. He knew he probably deserved to be fired just for that. Finally, this employee was extremely valuable to the firm and replacing him wouldn't be very easy. This employee felt he could do better but he couldn't come up with an alternative strategy that he felt comfortable with. He saw it coming.

Let's analyze the speech. It starts by using the phrase "as you remember," hinting that this conversation took place and the employee should recall it from the past, rather than be surprised. It then states that this conversation took place last week, making it easier for the employee to recall it. It uses the phrase "*your* choice of strategy" to indicate that this employee was accountable for making this decision. The speech then recaps the conversation from last week, pointing out both the CEO's and the employee's position. It then explains the reason why this employee is getting fired. Note how it doesn't say "you failed" or "you did" or "you were supposed to." Instead, it says the firm is going in the wrong direction. It didn't say "you are going in the wrong direction." The "we" in the sentence points out that it's a team effort. It also doesn't say "in the wrong direction," but rather says "in the direction other than." This phrasing makes this sentence less negative, perhaps neutral, if anything. The speech then points out that this employee has great ideas. This sentence serves several functions. First, it tells the employee that he is still worth something. Second, it explains the negative in a positive way. Third, it shows that it's a bad fit, rather than a screw-up (the word "aligned" makes it clear). Finally, this sentence tells the employee that he is getting terminated without using the ugly word "fired." The speech continues by stating there's an interview waiting and introducing the severance package, showing that the firm cares and wants to help the employee. It then takes a risk and asks for a smooth transition. This one is hard, since many employees would prefer to be put out of their misery immediately. But the final "good luck" reinforces the fact that the firm really does wish this employee well. In this particular case, this employee agreed to a smooth transition, thanked the CEO for the opportunity to serve, and spent the next 2 months making sure the new person who took over his job succeeded.

Now let's look at a conversation with a person who doesn't know where he or she stands. If you follow general advice of this book, your people will usually be prepared. But people are people. There may be exceptions. Plus you may have people you haven't really been up front with before you read this book. To make things easier, let's divide people into two groups: those who are surprised but are capable of comprehending why they are getting terminated, and those who will likely never get it.

If people don't know where they stand, you will obviously surprise them. Any sort of surprise may have a negative impact, especially when you deliver bad news. Many cases of damage caused by disgruntled employees are the direct result of this surprise. Therefore, this surprise should be delivered in a way that will limit harm to the organization. This includes a careful selection of the place and time (e.g., conference room next to the front door, or termination after hours), some up-front preparation work, and a careful selection of words. The up-front preparation may include a write-up and collection of facts to back up the termination. The words should be selected carefully in order to help the person understand the reason behind termination.

Because your employee doesn't know where he or she stands, the employee will probably be upset that he or she hasn't been provided sufficient feedback before. To minimize the destructive impact of surprised employees, one can follow the *strategy of one case.*

The strategy of one case is especially effective for employees who may not understand the feedback given to them. The basic idea behind this strategy is to focus the entire termination on one case of poor performance rather than the overall pattern. Once the case has been explained, the employer can describe the overall pattern of poor performance in a suggestive way. Consider the following speech:

> Jack, I called you in to discuss a concern I have. This morning you came in 2 hours late and you didn't notify me that you were running behind. Due to the critical nature of your job, our policy states that you must notify your supervisor if you can't make it on time. Because you violated our policy, we will part company today.

As you see from this speech, it addresses one specific instance of a problem rather than the whole pattern. If you were to start by saying you are not satisfied with employee's attendance, you would probably spend the next few hours debating whether this statement is valid, trying to produce evidence of this happening in the past and explain why you haven't brought this up earlier. By focusing on one instance of poor attendance, you put fewer discussion items in your employee's head, making it harder for him to debate your case. The case of being late "this morning" is easier to comprehend than the pattern. The employee likely remembers being late today. A conversation about a pattern of past lateness will probably look like this:

> *Employee*: What are you talking about? I've never been late. Give me an example!
> *Manager*: September 21 you came in 30 minutes late.
> *Employee*: I don't remember what happened on September 21. I am sure I wasn't late. If I was, I am sure I called you and notified you. Give me another example!
> *Manager*: How about October 1?

Employee: You are pointing out dates that happened months ago.
  I don't remember what happened. If this was an issue back
  then, why didn't you tell me right away?
Manager: Well, I have a record of you being 30 minutes late every
  morning the week of the 20th of November . . . This is more
  recent.
Employee: I was sick that week and you knew it! Why are you
  picking on me? You are obviously making it personal!

This conversation will go on and on and will never have the meeting of the minds. In fact, it's unreasonable to expect the employee to remember why he came in late 6 months ago. The whole conversation will annoy the employee and turn his mind against you, forcing him to deny every allegation, even if he knows it's the truth. When humans go into a defensive mode, they tend to dismiss every statement made. A conversation with a person in such mode is often fruitless. Even mentioning a single case of what happened "this morning" may be worthless at this point. A person in a defensive mode will find a justification for absolutely every decision he has ever made in his life.

Talking about a single case focuses all attention on one specific instance of a problem. Of course, a smart employee may link this morning's lateness to his or her attendance in general and follow up with a question asking why an issue of lateness hadn't been brought up before. Such a question will attempt to expand the focus from a single case to the overall pattern. Unless a manager has a reasonable explanation for why feedback hasn't been provided before, he or she should hold this conversation in control and try to stay focused on a single case. Here are sample come-back statements that will help you shift focus:

Jack, I really wish your previous supervisor had told you about this lateness in the first place. But I would like to be fair and only discuss issues I have firsthand knowledge of. So let's focus on what happened this morning.

Jack, I am glad you brought this up. I'll be happy to address previous cases once we discuss what had happened today.

You are right. I wish I gave you feedback before. It would probably be unfair for me to go over past issues if I hadn't been up-front with you. That's why I want to focus on the immediate issue and discuss what happened this morning.

The first statement comes from a manager who was just appointed into his or her position. He or she can claim ignorance of previous cases and show ignorance as being fair to the employee. The second sentence is the easiest one to deliver. It promises to address the employee's concerns and quickly shifts focus to a single case. The third one is similar to the second one. However, it has one advantage and one disadvantage. The advantage is that you show leadership by admitting your own mistake. The disadvantage is that admitting your own mistake may cause legal action against you. It may also open a can of worms and have a smart employee probe you even further. Use this one at your own risk!

Once you present your single case to an employee, it's only fair to give him or her additional feedback and show the overall pattern. In fact, terminating an employee for a single case without describing a pattern won't teach the employee what he or she needs to do differently in the future. You have to describe the pattern in a way that doesn't prompt any additional discussion but gives your employee enough food for thought. For example, you can say something like the following:

> In order to be more effective in the future, try to watch your attendance and how it's aligned with the company policy.
>
> I am glad you were able to see the issue we had this morning. Now that we've talked about it, I want you to consider previous cases of your lateness.

I had a client who terminated a technical employee for failing to install antivirus software on computers under his control. This employee believed exactly what he was told—he was terminated for not installing the antivirus software. After he had been terminated, he decided to always have the antivirus software installed and updated on every computer he ever touched. In this case, the employer successfully executed the first part of the strategy and communicated a single case of noncompliance with company policy. But this employer had failed to communicate the pattern. The fact is that this employee constantly violated company policy. But he was never told that. It wasn't about the antivirus. It was about the overall tendency to violate all rules. This employee will probably do the same thing for his next boss and then the one after that, until he finds a boss who will be honest with him.

Now let's suppose the person doesn't have the capacity to understand why he or she is being let go. One should be careful with making such a determination. If the termination speech is delivered properly, 95% of the people are capable of comprehending the issue. The 5% that doesn't grasp the issue most likely involves people with some kind of a mental disability, drug abuse issue, or some other deficiency. I've met very few people who fall into this category, but they represent interesting cases on their own. One such person was known to skip work to take her cat to the movies. One day she came to work late because her "cat was robbed of $100." She was very mad that no one believed her and made it a point that she even had a police report, which she managed to misplace. I've seen another person who at the age of 45 was still living with her mother and was dating a person 25 years younger than she is. She complained about sexual harassment against another employee for saying hello to her, stating he said hello to hit on her. She refused to pay taxes saying this was the government's way to cheat her out of her money and she didn't believe in paying taxes in the first place. Another employee was caught bullying his coworkers when their manager was absent, asking them to agree that he was their real boss. His justification for thinking that way was that he had a law degree.

People like this shouldn't have been hired in the first place. But for the purpose of this exercise, we should assume they were and now we have to let them go.

This type of termination is the hardest one to do. Having a conversation with this type of a person is meaningless, but if you don't talk to him or her, you will hurt the employee even more. In fact, a person with a mental disability will have a hard time finding another job. A person with a mental disability and over a certain age limit will have even harder time finding a job. A person with those parameters who also doesn't know why he or she was let go has almost no chance of finding a job, unless the person gets interviewed by an incompetent manager.

Since we've assumed that it is impossible to explain anything to these people, we need to create an alternative strategy. Let's call it *the other job strategy*.

Let's start by asking ourselves a question: How and why did we hire these people in the first place? When asked this question, most managers come up with one of these three answers:

1. I didn't know the person was like this.
2. I was desperate and couldn't find anyone else to do the job.
3. I didn't think it was going to be a problem.

Great managers who are able to confront reality can instantly see a pattern here—all three reasons have the same common source—lack of leadership. In fact, any leader's job is to put the right people in the right jobs. Managers who respond with any of the answers above need to learn how to better screen potential candidates and improve their hiring practices. If you do your job and place the right people in the right jobs, second and third answers shouldn't exist in your world.

But here's the positive side. Very few managers are educated enough to understand the leader's job well enough to not repeat your mistake. In fact, millions of other managers will hire this person for one of the three reasons stated above. What's worse (or better for the employee), is it will take these managers a while to realize any issues with the employee, if they realize them at all. Some of these employees will stay in the wrong jobs all their lives. Most will never realize it. But some will magically find the right job!

What this means is that letting people like this go isn't as bad as it seems. Sure, it will be harder for them to find another job than for most people, but jobs do exist for them.

If you look at the overall intent of firing people the right way, you will see that we do this to help the firm *and* the person being let go. Just like your other employees, these people aren't necessarily evil. They are likely in the wrong jobs. Just like your other employees, these people want to enjoy their lives and take jobs they like. So yes, there are jobs for them. That's where *the other job strategy* comes into play. The basic idea behind it is that it isn't much different from terminating your regular employees, except you reduce the focus on the final conversation and explanation of the termination reason and increase the focus on where they will go next and how great it is going to be. Because these people aren't capable of understanding their performance challenges, they won't understand them when expressed by the next employer either. It would be a waste of time to try to explain to them something they aren't capable of understanding, although mentioning the problem briefly may help in case legal action is ever brought against the employer. Unfortunately, one of the best ways for them to find a job that is a good fit is to try many jobs until they find the one they feel comfortable with. There are several psychological profiles that may help as well, the Kirton Adaptive Innovative Inventory (KAI)[9] being one of the most effective ones.

There are several ways to execute the *other job strategy*. Some are advisable, while others should never be followed. The following are examples of both:

Promote them. The famous Peter Principle states that every person gets promoted to the highest level of incompetence.[10] Many large companies follow this rule by promoting people they don't want. When people get promoted to the job that doesn't exist in the team, they get moved to another team, essentially handing off a bad employee to the next sucker. Although this method works for individual team members, it is really ineffective from the company perspective. The firm needs to put the best people in the right positions, not promote the wrong people to the wrong positions and then force them to perform. Some companies go a little too far with this strategy. One such company promoted a junior manager to a vice president role that didn't exist and laid the person off immediately afterward because the firm already had too many VPs. Another Fortune 50 company promoted a junior salesperson all the way to the senior vice president level. This person was then named CEO of another Fortune 50 firm and was fired shortly thereafter, resulting in a multibillion-dollar problem. It took almost a dozen promotions until someone realized that this person was several levels too high.

Help them voluntarily leave. I had a client who wanted to remove a person who just couldn't understand his performance issues. Conversations with this employee were senseless. My client found a solution. He found another company that was advertising a similar position. The candidate applying for this position would have to obtain security clearance[11] to perform work. Knowing that staff with security clearance typically make 20–30% more than regular people, this client "accidentally" spilled this information to the employee he wanted to leave. The bait worked. The poor-performing employee applied for and got the job. At the end of the day, there was no one to terminate. This approach proved very effective to this particular employer, although it is important not to engage in negligent referral when helping an employee to voluntarily leave.[12]

Build them up. While these people may not be able to understand performance problems, many can still be coached and developed. One of my clients designed a process allowing every employee to determine what he or she wanted to do with his or her career 1, 5, 10, or 20 years down the road. The company would then work with each employee to make the wishes come true, even if they went against the company's interests. Every employee knew and appreciated this noble approach. A person wanting to grow into a certain position would be given a time line and the list of tasks to complete. The firm would notify the employee if he or she would have to continue the job elsewhere once the employee grew into this position. This time line would be built far in advance, letting employees know of the possibility. Thus, when it was time for the firm to let employees go, employees looked at the move positively, thinking it was done in order to help them make the next big move. This may not be the best approach, but it was effective for employees who just couldn't understand what was expected of them.

As you can see, there isn't a clean and easy approach to terminating someone who doesn't get it. But when you design your strategy, think of some ways you can shift your conversation from why they are being terminated to how great their next job will be.

The Aftermath

Once your employee is terminated, you should follow the three steps described in this section.

Don't Keep It a Secret

When I say "don't keep it a secret," I don't mean you should antagonize or embarrass terminated employees. Instead, I am saying that managers should clarify that an employee termination has occurred and managers should state the reasons for the decision to terminate. Most employers hide the reason employees have been terminated. Some say absolutely nothing to the remaining staff; others make up a story or keep it short. A typical explanation is that the terminated employee had decided to move on or was simply "no longer here." Most managers believe that the less other employees know, the better. In reality, the opposite holds true. There are two main reasons employers must tell the truth to the remaining staff:

Reduce gossip. The less your employees know, the more gossip they will spread. This gossip will turn into a game of broken telephone with no reliable sources but lots of ideas. Some people will believe the gossip. It will turn into a collection of false facts and lots of talk behind your back. At some point, it may get out of control. The organization will experience shock from a nonexistent problem. I've seen masses of people go into depression, look for jobs, or quit because they believed they would get laid off soon. Another employee who was supposedly laid off was living proof of that. Not a single staff member was ever told that this employee was terminated for gross negligence. Not telling the truth caused a chain reaction, prompting hundreds of employees to leave the firm.

Educate employees. When people are terminated, this is your best opportunity to teach the remaining employees a lesson about expectations. You are in control if you tell the truth and deliver it in a believable way. This is what we mean when we say, "don't keep it a secret."

Being open about terminated employees shows that you are serious about your expectations and you are in control. But be honest here. Don't make up stories that benefit you. The truth is what makes a difference.

I was asked to help my client fix a poor-performing team consisting of approximately 15 senior-level people. I first evaluated their performance and found the root cause of the problem. There was no system of rewards and punishments. There was no culture of execution or system of follow-up. Employees not doing their jobs were never told that. Someone else would just do the job for them. Whenever they screwed up, they did nothing to fix the problem. Why fix anything if there is no punishment?

Here's what I did to fix this organization. First, I came up with the list of expectations in writing. This list was communicated to each member of the team. I would then hold meetings with the entire team and publicly ask them tough questions about their performance. When people didn't perform, I would take them out of the room and terminate them. I would then come back into the room and tell everyone the exact reason this employee was terminated. I quickly identified three employees who weren't supposed to be in the organization in the first place. These three employees were the best example of poor performance. I terminated all three and gave every member of the staff a very detailed explanation of why this was done. I overheard a conversation between two people after the first termination. One person stated that he will absolutely finish his project on time because he just saw that the organization was now serious about letting people go. After the three poor performers were terminated, performance level skyrocketed. It even came to the point that there was no reason behind a system of punishments.

If I were to terminate three employees and not communicate the reason to the rest of the team, this approach wouldn't work as effectively or wouldn't work at all. Employees would likely believe that these were layoffs or speculate around other reasons and then either look for jobs elsewhere or get disgruntled and perform even worse.

Sun Tzu,[13] a famous Chinese general who lived over 2,000 years ago, displayed a similar approach when he was asked to train a harem of 180 concubines as soldiers. According to the legend, Sun Tzu appointed the king's two most favorite concubines as officers. When he gave concubines a command to face right, they giggled. Sun Tzu then executed the two officers, to the king's protests. From that point on, the rest of the concubines followed every command he gave and became real soldiers.

As you can see, there's great benefit in being open and honest, but one should be careful. The main purpose is to create transparency, promote honesty, show your staff that you are serious, that you are in control, and that you mean what you say. The purpose is not to scare employees. Leaders don't scare people. Leaders lead people. Scared people may follow you, but they will use every opportunity to escape and won't be as productive as those who are truly led.

But be careful when you provide explanations. You may be found liable for things you say, so make sure you are honest and accurate. In the perfect would, you should also have documentation to back up anything you say. You might obtain legal advice as well.[14]

Make Sure They Haven't Hurt You

Terminated employees can cause no damage or can destroy your company. It's usually hard to predict what they will do. If you followed all the advice in this book and your employees knew about termination in advance, there's a good chance that you shouldn't worry about this section of the book. Either your employees won't try to harm you or it's already too late. But it's still a good exercise to consider your options.

Some employees set up time bombs,[15] believing this approach will ensure job security. Others will feed the remaining employees information that may hurt you or employee morale. I've witnessed a case of a terminated consultant who tried to hurt her consulting firm by sending out letters to the company's customers. After she had been fired for gross misconduct, she sent letters notifying customers about the firm's "questionable" accounting practices, such as false billing, invalid time reporting, and other things. The firm didn't do any of the things stated in letters, but it didn't matter. Some customers left, costing this firm millions of dollars.

While you can't prevent every problem, you can at least consider some of the simple ones.

Revoke all access. Some employers allow employees to go back to their desks, enter their office, or talk to employees after they've been fired. In order to prevent any problems, all security access must be revoked *before* you tell your employee about termination. This must include building access (keys, keycards, alarm or door pass codes, etc.) and computer access (disable users, change passwords, revoke rights, etc.). Your employees shouldn't be able to gain access to *any* resources in your company by the time you announce that they are being let go, including any of the remaining employees.

Draft a cease communications order. It's usually a bad idea for terminated employees to talk to the ones who remain with the firm. Remaining employees will hear things about you they shouldn't hear and your terminated employee will get information you wish he didn't get. One way to prevent such communication is to issue a cease communications order. The feasibility of this approach depends on the local law but it is known to be effective in many of the states in the United States. Written as a letter, this order tells the terminated employee that he isn't allowed to talk to any of the remaining employees. If he does, you can sue him for damages. You should not only issue a written order to the fired employee but also talk to your remaining employees. Explain the situation to them and ask them not to communicate with people who were let go.

Listen. If the wrong message gets to your employees, it may destroy your culture. Listen to your employees. Try to understand what they are discussing, what they believe in, and how they feel about what happened. Don't dismiss anything you hear. Once you hear something that bothers you, act upon it immediately!

Let them have unemployment. Fired people will already have hard times, typically due to either financial trouble or coping with the loss of their job. The last thing employers need to do is make it even worse for them by denying unemployment benefits. Yet many employers in the United States do just that, usually in order to keep their unemployment insurance premiums low. Although this makes sense to employers from the financial point of view, it creates much unneeded pressure on employees. These employees get upset when benefits are denied and turn into a powerful force that can destroy your brand, your culture, and your business. While most employees will quietly get upset and do nothing, there are many cases of employees filing lawsuits, delivering sensitive information to competitors, and communicating with your employees and your customers in an unwanted way. The cost of higher unemployment insurance premiums is much lower than the cost of damage these employees can cause.

Let them have that next job. Some employers will offer to serve as a reference to help people get that next job. Others will use that as an opportunity to tell potential employers about various problems this new candidate can cause. There may be several issues with either approach.

Giving a bogus reference in order to help people get that next job can make you and your firm liable to the new employer. There have been many cases in the United States of employers suing those providing phony references and winning large sums of money in damages. Plus it can make you legally liable for any damage done by the referred employee. Don't give fake references!

Unfortunately, giving truthful references can hurt you as well. First of all, you are stopping your employee from getting that next job. Remember, it may not be your employee's fault that he got fired, and it is probably your responsibility to help him find that next job. Second, there have been cases in the United States of employees suing their previous employers for giving negative references through defamation lawsuits, resulting in them not being able to obtain the next job. It's counterintuitive, but be careful with truthful references!

So if you can't give away fake references and you can't give away any truthful ones, what do you do? There're two approaches:

1. Don't give any references at all. Tell your terminated employees to not use you as a reference. If someone calls for a reference, refuse to give it. Some employers have a policy of not giving any references about any employee who left. If that's the policy you adopt, simply state that. However, you should consult an attorney every time you fire an employee. Court cases in the United States have held companies accountable for negligent referral even if they refused to provide information about the current or former employee. If you are aware of issues that could be materially important for the person's performance on the next job, you might need to disclose that information. For example, if you terminate a bus driver for drinking on the job and you refuse to disclose that to another bus company, you can be held liable if the employee crashes a bus while drunk.

2. Talk to your employee about a possible reference you can both agree on. Smart people understand that being let go doesn't necessarily mean that they are incompetent. Many people don't hide it but rather learn from their experience and evolve into a better self. If that's the type of person you are terminating, talk to him and try to agree on a positive reference that represents the firing as a learning experience.

I once had to interview a person who had been fired from his previous job. He quickly disclosed that. He said he made a mistake and told me what this mistake was. He also said he learned a lot from this misstep. He proceeded to talk, and I saw that he definitely had learned. When I called his boss for a reference, I got a positive confirmation of everything that occurred. The boss described it as "an unfortunate set of circumstances that forced me to let this employee go." He then proceeded to say that he's a great employee who surely learned a lot from this mishap and will perform well in the future. I ended up hiring this person and he did very well. If it weren't for his previous boss giving me an honest but positive reference, I possibly wouldn't have taken the risk to hire the person. If I didn't hire the person, his ex-boss could have suffered from potential lawsuits or badmouthing from the employee.

The bottom line is, let them have that next job!

Protect trade secrets. Most employees are given an offer letter when they begin employment. This offer letter states that employee promises to keep all company secrets confidential and not work for competitors or the same industry for a certain period of time. When people are terminated, they typically forget this rule. Watch where these employees go and what they say. If they started working for your competitor and you do believe they can share competitive information with them that will put you in a disadvantage, contact your attorney and see what you can do to stop that.

Follow Legal Advice

You should definitely follow legal advice both before and after the termination. Most managers believe they know the law and they have the power to terminate anyone for any reason. Yet countless lawsuits prove them wrong again and again. Consider the following examples:

Example 1

After being terminated for not performing his job, an employee sued his employer for not giving the employee precise instructions and training to perform the job properly. This employee won.

Example 2

A manager who was terminated sued the employer for racial discrimination. She stated she was the only African American on the team and she was the only one fired for not delivering the project on time. The fact that she was a manager in charge of a team and it was her responsibility to deliver the final product didn't matter. It also didn't matter that it was because of her that the team didn't deliver. She won the lawsuit and collected a nice chunk of change.

Example 3

A terminated employee sued her employer for not paying her overtime when she worked over 40 hours per week. It didn't matter that this employee was salaried.[16] She explained in court that she didn't understand what "salaried" meant and she was misled to believe she was getting paid extra for working nights and weekends. Although her employer produced strong evidence that she was educated about her salary and overtime pay, she won the lawsuit and collected money for all the overtime pay supposedly owed to her.

There are many other examples. Some problems could have been prevented if legal help was obtained before termination. While some employers would bring up high legal fees or unavailability of in-house counsel as justification for not consulting lawyers, they end up paying more when lawsuits are filed. Some employers are also driven by ego. In fact, most employers believe that they are right and that they processed termination correctly. Yet those exact employers are shocked when they lose legal judgments against them.

The bottom line is that you need to seek legal advice. Call your lawyer before you terminate your employee and consult on the reason as well as how you are going to do it. See if he or she can envision any challenges or harmful consequences with your method or your reasoning. You should also consult him or her after the firing to make sure you've done everything correctly and to see if you should do anything next.

Be careful with legal advice, though, and choose what guidance you follow carefully. Lawyers aren't managers. Their advice is rotated around their interpretation of the law, not the best management practices. If you hear advice that conflicts with your strategy, your management principles, or any recommendations given in this book, consider a happy medium or an alternative method. In some cases, it may be worth it to take legal risk. For example, lawyers will probably suggest that you never tell your employees that they were a bad fit in the company. This points out that it's your fault and your company's liability. While they are right and you may be found liable, chances of that happening are slim to none, especially when you are always candid with your team and you show great leadership. The payoff of being honest with your people far outweighs the risk of being sued for that.

Dealing With Angry People

No matter how good you are or how well you've worked out your system of firing, there will be those who get angry. This anger can be expressed by anything from looking upset to throwing pieces of furniture at you. Most employers try to reason with such people and explain their point of view.

That's their biggest mistake! Remember our conversation about people in defensive mode?[17] This one is even worse! Not only are they in defensive mode, but they are also angry about their situation. People in such a position blame what happened on anyone but themselves. Anything said to them at this point becomes an argument. And who typically wins an argument in cases like this? No one, because human beings always believe they are right! In other words, people who are angry that they just got fired listen to no one, blame everyone, and argue with everyone that they are right. Talking to people in this mode is completely senseless. Their defensive mechanism will find a counterargument for everything you say, including things everyone thinks are obvious. Real facts will be accepted as lies. Candid feedback will be taken as personal prejudice. Advice will be dismissed.

So what do you do with these people? There are two approaches.

Do nothing. In fact, you will probably get more use out of talking to the wall. Try to cut your exposure to such people short. Don't argue with them. Don't say anything. Don't respond in any way, either positive or negative. Just try to get them to leave as soon as possible. Anything you say will prolong the problem. Remember, talking to the wall at this point may be a better use of your time.

Make them feel better. This one is harder to do. This approach will prolong the conversation but will make your employee feel better, not because of how you respond but because you let him or her spill his or her guts. When people are upset, they want to talk. They feel better by complaining, sharing their feelings, or screaming. Let them. Don't interrupt. Don't defend yourself. Allow the employee to feel that he or she is right and you are wrong. Just let the employee say whatever he or she wants to say. Once the employee is done, politely escort him or her out. Make sure to do it the same way you'd escort the employee if he or she wasn't mad at you.

Neither of these approaches has any pluses for you, but the second one has a plus for the employee. Of course, this employee may still follow up with some nasty actions against you, but at least this approach will show the humane side of you. Plus it can be a good exercise of emotional intelligence.

One final word of advice: be careful with angry people. They are unpredictable. You may want to keep another person in the room with you during terminations to act as a witness and for security and safety reasons.

CHAPTER 3

Laying Off

Not Much Different From Firing

One gloomy morning I was sitting in the office with the CEO of a large company. His office was located on a beautiful campus that was home to this multinational firm and thousands of its employees. This morning was different from others. This CEO had just announced that his firm was laying off hundreds of people in order to cut administrative costs. "This is a pure financial decision," he explained. "My job is to increase shareholders' wealth, and I am doing that by reducing costs and making my firm more competitive." He proceeded to tell me how well he communicated his vision to the executive team. Everyone bought into his idea. Everyone agreed it was only for the best.

I looked outside through his floor-to-the-ceiling tinted window. Groups of people were loading boxes with personal belongings into their cars. Everyone was quiet. People looked as murky as the morning. The afternoon promised to be sunny, but the forecast for people didn't look as promising.

I remembered the words of the CEO: "Everyone agreed it was only for the best." I looked at him and asked, "Whose best?"

He smiled. "The company, of course," he replied. He took a sip of water from his glass. "It's my job to do what's good for the firm."

"How do you know it's good for the firm?" I asked.

"Because I'll cut costs. I've discussed this with my team and they've agreed with me," he responded.

"Have you discussed it with the people you just let go?" I asked.

He looked at me as if I just fell from the moon. "Who the hell cares? They are gone now," he responded. "I don't have the will nor time to talk to them. What will change if I talk to them?"

"What about people who stayed with the firm?" I asked.

"Companies lay off people all the time. Everyone knows why this happens. What else is there to say?" he replied.

This was a typical mistake CEOs make. The news of the layoff spread quickly. People who were terminated called the ones who stayed to complain about their situation. The power of rumors turned a minor cost-cutting exercise into a powerful machine of people turned against their own company. Some believed it was just the beginning of a much bigger personnel cut. Others thought the firm was being sold or was going bankrupt. People lost trust in their employer. Those who were loyal now believed they were betrayed. Hard workers no longer wanted to perform work for the company that was supposedly going to lay them off next. Customer service folks spent more time discussing rumors with their clients than issues. Customers started leaving. Product quality degraded. Employees started leaving. New candidates didn't want to join the firm. The brand that once stood for quality, reliability, and good customer service now stood for chaos and broken promises. What looked like a $23-million cost-cutting exercise became a multibillion-dollar problem that put the entire company at risk. Ultimately it cost the firm over $100 million to restore trust in the company.

The CEO was right that companies lay off people all the time. But he didn't know how to do it right. The reality is that a layoff isn't much different from firing, especially if it's delivered as a surprise. People get upset. Gossip starts. It travels far and destroys the company from the inside like cancer. External lawsuits from laid-off employees become a costly annoyance.

What makes a layoff most similar to firing is the aftereffect of losing one's job. It doesn't matter if the employees lost jobs due to cost cutting (which is supposedly good for the firm!) or because they performed poorly. The bottom line is that tomorrow their day will start in an unemployment line. Considering that over 47% of all the employees in the U.S. live paycheck to paycheck to make ends meet,[1] this also means immediate financial trouble for a lot of them, even those making over $100,000 per year.[2] Regardless of how the layoff has been handled, these people are in a state they don't want to be in. They are now a powerful brand-destroying machine waiting to explode. This machine requires control!

Those who have had to fire people but haven't had the opportunity to lay anyone off often think that laying off people is easier than firing. In fact, firing involves having tough conversations, interacting with legal folks, explaining what people did wrong, and possibly completing tons of paperwork to back up the decision. Laying off is easier. Just tell people you are doing it for the best of the firm. Surely they will understand, right? The real world example from the beginning of this chapter shows otherwise! This is why many layoffs don't yield the financial benefits expected by executives.[3]

Losing a job isn't fun, regardless of reasons. Here's an exercise. Pretend you were just laid off from your current job. You live paycheck to paycheck, have zero savings, and were eagerly waiting for that paycheck next week to cover the cost of your son's root canal. Your spouse is a full-time, stay-at-home parent. Your daughter just asked you for money to buy a prom dress. You need to feed your family until you find that next job. Your landlord won't take an "I owe you" and expects a payment by the end of next week. He calls the sheriff's office to prepare to evict you and your family. On top of all that, your car just broke down, so you can't go to an interview. You now have to choose between eating, paying rent, or fixing your car.

Questions

1. How does this make you feel?
2. Do you care why you lost your job?
3. Do you care that you are in this position for the good of the company?
4. Do you care that you were laid off and not fired?
5. What feelings do you have for your employer?

While it's hard to answer these questions precisely without really getting laid off first, it gives you a good idea of what goes on in the head of a person who was just been laid off. That's why a layoff should be treated similarly to firing. That's why it's important to handle it right!

While you can't predict and prevent every problem, you can at least reduce your exposure to negative consequences by using the framework we will be discussing further in this book. It works by reducing or completely eliminating aggravations that cause employees to destroy your organization.

There can be several levels of aggravation. They can range from minor annoyances to irritation to deep stress. Let's identify some sources of aggravations. Depending on the person, they may include the following.

1. Loss of income
2. The loss of money to cover immediate financial needs
3. Feelings of betrayal
4. Feelings of a personal failure
5. The uncertainty of the future
6. Feelings of disrespect
7. Feelings of unfair treatment

The subsequent chapters of this book will look at some of these sources of aggravation and explain how their effect can be reduced or how they can be eliminated completely.

Transparency

Managers who lay off people all the time will tell you that surprising people is key. If people expect layoffs, they may quit the company early, leaving you without much needed resources to finish certain projects. Some may set up time bombs, spread unwanted rumors, or even show up at work with a gun. While there's some truth to this, surprising employees may cause you to face even bigger challenges. Plus, issues such as time bombs and rumors can be prevented, if managed properly.

Transparency is the ultimate remedy that reduces these aggravations. It doesn't mean you should tell your employees that they'll lose their jobs next week. Instead, you should let your employees know how your company is doing and what its strategy is so your employees can foresee when those layoffs may occur.

Consider the following example. My client had a division that was in a poor financial situation. This division had been losing money for several years in a row. Both short- and long-term outlooks appeared to be unpromising. The firm had decided to sell this division to a competitor.

As a result of this sale, most employees would get laid off. Being the biggest advocate of transparency, the CEO of this firm communicated financial results and his intents to all employees across all divisions. Financial performance had been shared with all employees every single year the firm had been in existence. This CEO discussed his vision, mentioned the bleak outlook, the risks, and what he intended to do to remediate any problems. He mentioned that the scope of the problem was this division alone. He timely reported on every decision and every outcome. He asked employees to stick with him to make the company work, but he also mentioned he'd understand if employees looked for other jobs. He promised to pay extra to those who stuck around. While this approach didn't make employees happy, it created an opportunity for the most income-sensitive people to look for jobs while they continued working for the firm. They smoothly transitioned to their new jobs. Those who were less income-sensitive or entrepreneurial stayed with the firm and got a nice severance package when they were eventually laid off.

Let's look to see how this CEO handled aggravations. No one had a feeling of betrayal. Everyone believed the CEO and his teams were doing everything possible to save this division. Those who cared about money left early enough that it didn't become an aggravation. People felt respected because there was no element of surprise. Uncertainty about the future didn't matter as much because people were still gainfully employed when they found out about future layoffs, giving them enough time to find another job.

This firm didn't have to worry about time bombs, disgruntled employees, or destroyed brands either. These types of problems happen when people think of ways to get revenge for something the firm did to them. But there was nothing to get revenge for. They could clearly see that the firm tried its best to keep these employees and even promised generous severance packages to those affected. There was no rumor mill. People working in other divisions knew about their transparent CEO and they trusted him. They knew that the problem was limited to one division.

This particular example caused absolutely no stir in the organization. This firm sold its division to another company that quickly laid off 300 people who came with it. Very few of these people had any negative feelings about the firm. Neither the selling nor the buying firm has seen any damaging impact due to the layoff. All this was possible due to one thing: transparency.

In order to achieve the desired level of transparency, the firm should go by the following two concepts.

Honesty. Describe the situation to your staff exactly as it is. Notify them up front. Give them as much information as possible. Tell them what may or may not happen. State any risks. Tell them what you are doing about it. Suggest what they can do about it.

Employee participation. It's not enough to tell people what the state of the firm is. Many will believe it was management that put the firm in this position. They will continue blaming their bosses for what has happened. It's only human to blame everyone but themselves. In order to change their thinking, let them participate in the turnaround process. Tell them exactly what they have been doing and what they need to do. If they fail, they will feel like it's been in their hands all this time.

Consider the following example. I had a client whose business was shrinking due to heavy competition. His salespeople were losing customers. Both product capabilities and quality were inferior to that of his rivals. He was looking for a turnaround strategy. What made things worse is that he was short on capital, which was much needed to improve the product. He knew he had enough cash to survive up to 6 months.

The CEO went out with a message to his staff. He first addressed research and development (R & D) folks. He told them the product was inferior to that of the competition and salespeople couldn't sell it effectively. He asked them to think of innovative ways to improve the product. He further explained that failing to do so would mean that the firm would go out of business. He then went out to his sales team and told them that the firm was short on cash and was going to fold unless they can start meeting their quota. He went to marketing folks and challenged them with improving their product positioning efforts and rebranding products to better serve a lower end part of the market. He explained to them that failure to come up with a new winning marketing strategy would kill the firm.

This CEO followed up with each team every 2 weeks to give them an update. He gave people further guidance on things they could do. The company's financials were publicly distributed throughout the firm. The CEO publicly slashed his own salary to zero.

This strategy created a powerful force of people fighting for their lives. This company implemented more innovative ideas in the next 2 months than it did in the decade prior. The firm reorganized itself in such a way that 6 months of cash lasted it almost 2 years.

Unfortunately, the competition was fierce and very well funded. The firm didn't make it and had to let people go. But people didn't come out of it angry. They knew they tried their best and they were at fault for failing. They saw company financials and observed that their CEO led by example. They felt they were a part of a big effort to save the firm and they were glad to participate.

Of course, these employees weren't happy. After all, they lost their jobs. But not a single one said anything bad about the firm or considered revenge, time bombs, or anything destructive. The most they felt was that it was a shame to have failed.

Other than having great leadership skills, this CEO did three things that made a difference: he communicated frankly, he got his team to follow him by participating in fixing the problem, and he disclosed problems early enough in the process that they weren't yet viewed as problems, but rather as concerns. Had he told his staff about problems a day or a week before layoffs, it would have been too late. But he brought them up many months before they became evident. By bringing up potential problems and by letting people participate in the process, this CEO united his company and empowered employees to significantly improve their performance.

By being a part of the organization and decision-making process, employees understood what was going on, knew what to expect and what to do, prepared for the worst, and supported what the company was doing. The financially sensitive ones and those who were fearful about uncertainties went out to look for new jobs immediately. The less financially sensitive ones stayed. But even those who departed didn't say anything bad about the firm. As a matter of fact, most people didn't even notice their departure.

As you can see, transparency can go a long way, especially if it's well communicated from the very beginning, way before problems are obvious. In fact, having transparency as an integral part of your culture can prevent many other challenges. Some of the more successful firms embed transparency into their culture to such extent that nothing more needs to be communicated to people when problems occur. Company business is everyone's business every day, not just on a problem day.

Dignity

Chapter 2, "Firing," talked about dignity at length. But it deserves mentioning again and for a slightly different reason. Of course, all of the previous reasons we've discussed are still valid. You want to preserve culture, reduce communication problems, preserve your brand, and be humanistic.

But here's another semiphilosophical thought. While people you fire may have deserved to be dismissed in one way or another, those you lay off didn't. Of course, if you remember the reasons people get fired, you will question whether anyone deserves to be terminated at all. But here the situation is clear. You are not letting them go for who they are and for where you placed them. They are being let go because of financial decisions your company should make in order to survive. If you let them go because your company didn't make it, it's probably your fault for leading it in the wrong direction or for making poor choices. If this layoff occurs because you are cutting costs, it's your fault for hiring them in the first place. If your company didn't make it because your employees screwed up or didn't perform their job as expected, it's your fault for placing the wrong people in the wrong positions or for not giving them enough direction to perform correctly.

However you put it, it is likely your fault. You owe it to your staff to let them go with dignity. You can't blame someone for your own mistakes, especially if you are in a position of power over your employees' future.

I have a friend, let's call him John, who went through an exercise that shows exactly why preserving dignity is important. When I met him, he was working as a vice president in charge of a $100-million division of a large firm. His division was sold to another firm and he was laid off. The CEO of the acquiring company showed no respect for John and completely mishandled the layoff. John ended up on the street. He quickly found a job working for a competitor. This competitor decided to acquire John's previous employer within weeks of the layoff and put John in charge. The first thing John did was terminate the CEO of the newly acquired firm, showing him the same level of respect as he was once shown. He then proceeded to terminate most of the senior management team, who showed no respect for John at the time of his layoff.

What goes around comes around. These executives got punished for what they did to John, although they will probably never understand how John felt when he got terminated and why he came back to them with revenge.

There are many other reasons to preserve dignity. Just think of the situation you put the person in when you lay him or her off: unemployed, without any income, plenty of bills, and a family to feed. And it wasn't even his or her fault.

So how do you preserve dignity? Most employers believe they do it pretty successfully simply by telling the person he is being let go and quietly walking him out of the building. But terminated people think differently. Remember, they are in a defensive mode! These people get irritated by every detail: the way you talk to them, the way you called them into your office to tell them about termination, the size of their severance package, and even how you dress. Here are some quotes I've recorded from people who were laid off:

> Can you believe he laid me off on a Wednesday? How come he couldn't do it on Tuesday, before I decided to go shopping?

> My idiot boss called me to say that my position is getting eliminated because of the company's poor financial situation. Guess what he was wearing? Armani! He gets paid too much money to cover his expensive taste in clothes; that's why the company is going out of business and that's why I lost my job!

> And you know what he offered me in return for letting me go? Six months' worth of pay! Is that all I am worth to him? It's not that I need the money. I can find another job in a month, but it's ridiculous that he thinks so low of me.

A clear-minded observer would probably say that all three statements are absurd. Yet these statements were made nonetheless. Most likely they were made because employees were irritated. One may think this has nothing to do with dignity, so here's the thought. Dignity is about respect. It's not about what you do to show respect but about how people perceive it. You may do what you think is right, but people will perceive it negatively and think you were disrespectful.

Preserving dignity has a lot to do with understanding how your employee feels and how he responds to certain events. Of course, losing one's job pushes employees to the extreme of their defensive behavior, making their actions hard to predict.

One of the most important qualities of leaders is awareness of the impact of one's actions on other people. When you follow advice given further in this book, consider the impact of your actions on people. How do your actions impact the dignity of those you let go?

Although there's no *clear* prescription for preserving dignity, this approach will at least minimize the negative impact of its loss.

Thank Employees

This seems obvious, but many employers forget to thank their employees for work well done. If you think about it, your employees probably did a great job; otherwise you would have fired them.

Thanking employees is one way to show respect (think preserving dignity) and assure them that they are able to get another job. It's not a simple "thank you" that counts but the entire final speech you give them, which, by the way, must come from the heart.

Consider these two examples.

Example 1

"Jane, unfortunately our company isn't doing well so we must let you go. Thanks for the job well done, by the way."

Example 2

"Jane, I can't begin to tell you what a beautiful job you've done. You have truly great skills. You amaze me with your performance every day and I think you will succeed anywhere. The challenge is that our company isn't doing as well . . ."

The first example states the negative fact: you are terminated. It then adds a "thanks" in a way that looks like it was forced. This is especially evident when you add "by the way" at the end of the sentence, making it look like it was an afterthought. What makes it even more difficult is that no one will listen to your thanks. The first part of your speech already has your thoughts headed in a different direction.

The second example does a couple of things differently. First, it brings up the positive before the negative, reducing the level of downbeat feelings. Secondly, it thanks the person from the heart and uses a careful selection of words to show the person that it's not a simple "thank you." Finally, it follows by reassuring the person that everything will be OK, since her great performance will surely help her find that next job in no time.

A simple "thank you" can make the difference between an upset but grateful employee and one who will file that next lawsuit against you or tell your customers what a horrible firm he used to work for. Consider the following phrases I overheard from employees who were laid off:

They laid me off after I've done so much for them! What an ungrateful bunch of assholes!

I don't know if they laid me off or fired me. They never told me if I did a good job. They just told me they couldn't afford my services anymore.

The first statement could have been satisfied by simply stating how much this person was appreciated. Instead, this particular person filed a lawsuit for wrongful termination. Although she didn't win, it cost the firm a lot of money and headache to fight it.

I heard the second phrase from an employee undergoing a job interview. This employee will take a long time to find another job, since many employers won't risk hiring him with a questionable history like this. This employee may not be thinking badly about his previous employer today, but his view may change if he can't find another job in the next year or so. His employer failed to tell him why exactly he was let go and assure him that it wasn't him who was at fault by simply thanking him. Of course a simple "thank you" wouldn't be enough. Some employers would express gratitude to anyone just because it's their nature or because they feel uncomfortable telling their employee the truth. The real "thank you" must sound like it's coming from the heart. The manager delivering the message should be trusted and respected.

You should definitely express your gratitude to people. It doesn't cost you anything to do it right but it may cost you dearly if you do it wrong.

Help Employees

As we've mentioned several times before, we have to remove aggravations in order to prevent future problems. A lot of these aggravations are due to the situation you put your employees in: They are now unemployed, without money, possibly with some debt and a family to feed, and uncertain about the future. And of course it wasn't their fault that they got laid off. While we can't remove the root cause of these aggravations completely, we can at least perform some actions in that direction.

Give the Employees Money

Almost half of the people you lay off will be short on money the moment you let them go. The other half will feel uncomfortable knowing their source of income is gone. You can help these people by giving them some money that will last them while they are looking for a job. This onetime payment is usually referred to as severance. Different companies adopt different severance policies. Most will offer 2 weeks of pay to anyone they let go. Some will offer more. Others will offer none. A few companies will develop a complex formula, guaranteeing a certain severance package based on the person's tenure or position within the firm.

While any package is better than none, there are strategies for selecting what goes into severance pay. Here are some pointers.

How long does it take to find a job? A brief market survey for this employee's job will tell you how long this person will stay unemployed. In late 1990s, good software engineers in the Washington, DC, area could find another job in less than a day. In 2009 the time went up to approximately 2 weeks. A 2-week severance in 1990s could have been overkill but would be about right in 2009. For some positions it may be harder to establish the time to get another job. For example, a musician playing in the symphony orchestra may take years to find another job. A lot of them will end up looking for over a year and then get a job teaching. You can't give them years of severance, but you can estimate how long it will take to find a teaching job or how much money they will need to survive while they are looking.

How valuable was this employee? There is a difference in opinion whether an employee's value should matter when severance pay is given. Some will argue that giving some people more money than others is discriminatory. However, giving your star employees more money is only fair. In addition, such strategies can remove the unneeded aggravations. One employee I spoke with complained to me about his experience when he was laid off. He spent 20 years with the firm and got the same severance as another person who started less than a year before the layoff. He was loyal to his employer and felt that his loyalty had to pay off. He told me he understood exactly why the firm had to let people go and he agreed with its decision. His only aggravation was with the final treatment of company's veterans. A larger severance pay would have been beneficial in his case.

What is the risk of giving them less? Some employees present greater risk when they are laid off than others. Consider the difference between laying off a manufacturing worker and a senior executive. Both can sue the firm for damages. However, an angry executive *may* win 5, 10, or 20 times more than the manufacturing worker based on his salary, the amount he lost, the availability of funds to cover legal expenses, and the willingness of an attorney to participate in this case. I observed a layoff where junior managers received a 2-week severance while their division president got 1 year's worth. The company's lawyers thought that junior staff presented little to no legal risk while this division executive had the capability of suing for and winning up to 20 times his annual salary. This executive was offered severance in return for signing a document promising he won't litigate.

How much is too much? Don't bankrupt the company. Unless you are shutting down the company or its division, the purpose of the layoff is generally to cut costs. Yet some companies offer severance that far outweighs financial benefits. One company paid off 6 months' worth of salary to its laid-off employees only to hire most of them back within 3 months of the layoff. Another one was trying to raise $100 million in savings by cutting personnel but ended up paying $125 million in severance.

Additional benefits. Some firms offer financial benefits in addition to money. They may include free or discounted health insurance, usage of the corporate gym membership, a company-paid cell phone, a laptop, or a forgiven loan. These things look like tiny details but they matter a lot to people who just lost their jobs.

One should definitely be fair when delivering severance to terminated employees. I had a client who was trying to sell a division of the company. Dozens of employees scared for their jobs were leaving every day. In order to stop this mass exodus, the company offered employees a guaranteed 3 months' severance if their jobs got terminated. Believing the company, many employees stayed. However, when this division was finally sold, the new owner of the division laid off people based on his own rules, paying a 2-week severance. This created a mass consultation with labor attorneys. Unfortunately, this case went nowhere. However, it did create thousands of unhappy people, many of whom made it their personal goal to destroy this firm. Nine months after this layoff, the new employer had filed for bankruptcy. While most people linked this employer's trouble to financial mismanagement, their biggest problem was the improper management of people.

Help Employees Find Another Job

This seems like a tough task, and most employers don't even think about it. But your job is to remove those aggravations from people, and these aggravations won't go away until people find new jobs. And if you are the one responsible for them losing their jobs in the first place, it is your duty to help them find that next gig.

Some successful companies have developed a process of doing just that. There are instances of companies calling competitors to see if they can pick up people they let go. Some large firms operate or partner with unemployment centers, where they train people on new skills and teach them how to write effective resumes and pass job interviews. Some own staffing agencies that try to place people in other firms. Managers who are great networkers can make a few phone calls to their contacts and find jobs for key personnel. Some companies hire outplacement consultants who handle the whole process from layoff conversation to everything in the job transition process. These consultants can conduct seminars to help laid-off employees get a jump start on finding a new job and offer one-on-one consults to support employees in their job search process.

Regardless of how hard it is for you to help them, it is your obligation to do so.

References

We discussed references in the section about firing people. References for laid-off people are different. While not giving a reference for someone who was fired may be a good idea to help both the firm and the employee, not giving it when you laid someone off is generally cruel. Don't forget, it's your responsibility to help them find that next job! Giving a reference is a part of that. When you don't give a reference, you put a seed of doubt in the prospective employer's head, making it very hard for the employee to find that next job.

Giving a bad reference isn't great either. Some employers laid off people who were supposed to be fired and now want to tell the truth about the employee's negative performance to prospective employers. If that's the case, why not also tell the truth to the employee? They deserve to hear it as much as the new employer does. This new employer may forget your feedback the moment you give it, but your employee will suffer for a long time, unable to find another job. Employees with poor performance records should be fired, not laid off.

Do provide references for laid-off employees as much as possible. Make sure to disclose anything that may bother this new employer, such as the fact that it was a layoff, not a firing. Mention that you'd hire this employee back if you could. But don't lie! Tell them as it is!

The Process

Every company should have a process developed describing actions to take when people should be laid off. This process should be developed far in advance, before the company even considers letting anyone go. Since many things may go wrong during the layoff, this process should be well designed and practiced. How will you deliver the news? What do you offer your people? How do you help them cope? How do you walk them out? What legal actions must you take?

Let's look at some of those tasks more closely.

Choose the Right Words

Saying good-bye to your employees is hard, especially when they did nothing wrong. It's even harder if you've worked with these employees for an extended period of time and you feel like they are a part of your family. Thinking about consequences of the layoff for these people makes it seem impossible to let them go. Yet you have to lay them off and you have to choose the right words. Why do you need the right words? Because it helps you reduce aggravations, as described in the "Not Much Different From Firing" section of this chapter, and ultimately preserve your culture and your brand.

Let's start by looking at the framework of your talk. Your talk should include the following components.

The truth. As described in the "Transparency" section of this chapter, truth can go a long way. If presented properly, it can remove a lot of aggravations. Even if presented improperly, truth is important. People want to know why they are being let go, even though the reason doesn't really make a difference.

Expression of gratitude. Thanking your employees for the job well done shows respect and gives them assurance that there's something better out there for them.

Inspiration. It's hard to inspire people who just lost their jobs, but if you don't try, they will get depressed and turn into a powerful destructive force that can go a long way.

Respect. You have to help people preserve their dignity. They deserve nothing less.

Fairness. You have to ensure that people feel the process is fair.[4] People deserve to be fairly treated and, if you leave them feeling unfairly treated, survivors are more likely to reduce commitment or quit. Also, the ones losing their jobs are more likely to retaliate by suing you, sabotaging the company and/or the process, and speaking ill of your organization.

Next steps. Shift their focus from the current negative situation to something more positive, such as a better job.

Proper length. You don't want to be too brief. Simply telling people that their services are no longer needed isn't enough. They need to hear why. But don't go overboard. No one wants to hear a 30-minute speech. And if you follow the general advice of this book and do it right, this speech will probably be very short because people will already see it coming.

In addition, your talk should contain carefully selected words. If not chosen properly, these words can act as aggravators on their own. For example, there's a magic word: "challenge." Although carrying a negative meaning, it usually sounds positive. Compare the following phrases:

- Unfortunately our company isn't doing well.
- But our firm isn't doing well.
- The problem is that our firm isn't doing well.
- The challenge our firm is facing is that it isn't doing as well as expected.

Words such as "but" and "unfortunately" always sound negative, even if used in a positive context. The word "challenge" changes the meaning to be positive. What can make it sound even more positive is if you change a simple negative phrase to that of a comparison. Instead of saying "isn't doing well," use "isn't doing as well as expected." Although you are saying the same thing, the more positive approach carries a better aura, reducing the chances of your employee getting aggravated.

Some managers are perfectly happy using negative words, thinking they are a better descriptor of the truth. In fact, candor is an important quality here. But no one is debating the value of candor. You are not lying when you pick more positive words. You are simply removing the unneeded level of aggravation that your people don't deserve. There is no benefit of using negative words, only irritation.

Your talk should be written specifically for your scenario. Here's an example of a talk one of my clients had to give. It is simple and effective. There were no instances of disgruntled employees or aggravation that caused this firm any harm.

Thank you, everyone, for coming here on short notice. The reason I called you in is to discuss a challenge our firm is facing. As you know, we've just lost 30% of our customers to competition. Everyone worked very hard to prevent this high level of customer turnover, and I'd like to thank everyone for what they did. Our challenge is that the loss was still higher than the firm could handle. This put our firm in a situation requiring us to make significant cost cuts, including reduction in personnel. These cuts affect everyone in this room. In order to assist you with your job search, the firm will give each one of you a check equal to 2 months' pay and will cover your health insurance costs for the next 6 months or until you find the next job. I can't stress how thankful I am for what you did for the firm. I feel proud that I have worked with a team of talented people such as you. The great thing is that the current job market conditions are wonderful in our neighborhood because the government just increased spending on military software technology, which, as you know, is designed in our business park. As many as 3,000 new jobs will be created in this area in the next 2 months. What makes me even more excited about it is that the shortage of qualified personnel in this vicinity will drive salaries up by 30% to 40%. This gives me great confidence that each and every one of you will be gainfully employed and making even more money than you were here before your severance runs out. I'd like to thank everyone one more time and wish everyone good luck.

No speech is ever perfect, especially when you deliver bad news, such as news affecting one's perceived financial stability. Nor is it easy to deliver, no matter how well it's written. But the main purpose of our speech isn't to show our oratory skills, but rather to execute this step of the process with the minimum number of aggravations. Let's look at the previous example to see what concepts can reduce aggravations. At first, this speech looks simple. But it's the little details that can make a difference.

First, this speech begins with the truth. Employees already knew where the company stood. There was no element of surprise, just a recap of what they already knew. Of course, if this company were to practice a very high degree of transparency and get employees involved in some of its decision making, the speech wouldn't be needed at all. The company could tell employees up front that they will lose their jobs if the firm loses customers.

Second, this speech thanks employees several times. It's often good to repeat the words of gratitude more than once as they can be lost behind other words in your speech. But don't go overboard with it. At some point it will only be annoying to people. Note how the speaker mentions that he will provide employees with severance. To some people, this may be a sign of thanking them.

Third, this speech shifts focus to next steps and tries to motivate employees at the same time. Instead of spending time talking about the negatives, it talks about how great the future looks—better jobs paying more money that will be available very soon. Note the phrase "this gives me great confidence" It reinforces positives feelings and automatically sets a goal for employees to find new jobs within a couple of months. By using the phrase "I feel proud that I have worked with a team of talented people," the speaker thanks his employees one more time and motivates them by pointing out their abilities.

Fourth, this communication uses positive keywords and phrases. It uses "challenge" instead of "problem." It uses "high level of customer turnover" instead of "customers are leaving us left and right." By saying, "loss was higher than the firm could handle" instead of "we lost too much money" or "we don't have the money to pay for," it points out the issue at hand, makes listeners active participants in the discussion without placing fault on them, and communicates the message in a more positive way. Instead of saying "layoffs" or "firings," it says, "reduction in personnel." No one likes the words "layoff" or "firing." The word "wonderful" describing the current job market conditions reinforces positive feelings in people. By saying, "what makes me even more excited," the speaker points out how great new opportunities will be. Not good, but great! The sentence stating that this employer has great confidence in future job search success is reassuring as well, especially when it comes from a true leader. In general, the word "confidence" is very comforting when coming from someone people trust and follow.

Finally, the speaker wishes his employees good luck. This helps preserve their dignity and shows that the firm cares about their future success.

Keep in mind that each talk should be written according to the firm's current state of affairs and the audience to be laid off. Not all employees know the current financial situation the company is in. Not all are capable of understanding how their jobs are impacted. Some of them don't want to know. Explaining to a factory worker why he needs to be laid off after a guy in marketing screwed up on the SWOT[5] analysis or didn't analyze all of the Porter's Five Forces[6] will probably have no positive effects. But hiding the truth isn't the answer either. One should find the right language to deliver the message to any audience. For example, suppose your marketing executives made a mistake with the Porter's Five Forces and didn't build the right barriers of entry into your business, resulting in competition smashing your business. Instead of mentioning people in marketing, Porter, and barriers of entry, you can simply say, "Our competitors found a way to beat us by building a better product."

You wouldn't be lying by stating it this way, but you state it in a way most people understand. Notice how you don't mention the root cause of the problem. It's good to mention the root cause to people that have caused the problem. It will only make your life easier as they'll already know the outcome of their mistakes. Mentioning it to unrelated people will only cause a number of aggravations driven by uneducated biases. The last thing you need to hear following your speech is "Oh, it's those people in marketing that did it. I'll show them!" Any time people can point out the root cause as other than them, it results in an aggravation and a potential source of problems.

Be very careful with the words you pick. Every word can be taken negatively and used against you in the future. I've seen one example of an executive who used the words "early retirement" when he laid off some of his people. These people sued him for age discrimination. They alleged that he only laid off people in a certain age bracket. The words "early retirement" were the proof. Another executive laid off staff who "didn't share the cultural views of the firm." What he meant is that he established rules he expected people to follow in order to deliver exceptional customer service to the firm's clients. These people sued him for religious discrimination, alleging that "cultural views" he was referring to meant they weren't of the same religion as he was. They won.

As you can see, words mean a lot. Choose them wisely or they may end up being your last words.

The Walk-Out Process

Various organizations practice different methods of walking people out of the building once they've been laid off. Some take it slowly. They let people leisurely collect their belongings, walk around the building, say good-bye to their colleagues, smoke a cigarette, and complain about life.

Other firms walk people out the same way they'd escort criminals. Both approaches have pros and cons and neither is perfect.

In order to develop the most efficient process, one can combine the best of both worlds. To do so, one should define the objectives of a proper walk-out process. At a minimum, the objectives should be as follows.

1. We should minimize employees' aggravations.
2. We should reduce the risk of having potentially annoyed employees on the premises.
3. We should reduce communication between those who are leaving and those who are staying with the firm.
4. We should cut off the flow of information to employees who are leaving.
5. We should reduce the stress the layoff causes on the management and operations personnel who have to administer it.

Finding the balance of both worlds is tough. On the one hand, employees want the freedom to take time to collect their belongings. On the other hand, the longer they stay in the building, the greater the risk of unwanted events occurring and the greater the stress on management personnel. But this healthy balance must be found.

One of my customers found a way by laying off employees after hours. This customer operated a factory with all employees working exactly until 5:00 p.m. Because these were hourly workers and due to the company culture, most employees left work not a minute after 5:00 p.m. Around 4:30 p.m., my customer asked factory workers who were to get laid off to come to the conference room at 4:55 p.m. for a brief meeting. Employees were told they were being let go. Managers then spent the next 10 minutes talking about how the firm was to going to assist displaced workers with new jobs. When the meeting was over, the rest of the employees were already gone. When laid-off employees left the conference room to pick up their belongings, they didn't even notice the presence of security personnel who were watching as employees were leaving.

This particular layoff was successful. First, there were no employee aggravations. This employer happened to give them 6 months' worth of pay, as negotiated with the union. The executive doing the layoff gave a nice speech, motivating employees to find something more stable, reminding them that they did a wonderful job and they only lost their positions with the firm due to competitive forces outside of everyone's control. This speech was given in the presence of highly respected union leaders, who stood next to the executive doing the layoff and thanked employees for their hard work. These union leaders were well aware of the situation way before the layoff due to the great relationship this employer developed with them.

Second, this employer set up security personnel to monitor employees' exit in a nonintrusive way. This was a great strategy. Security was able to protect company assets without annoying employees.

Third, there was no contact between those who left and those who stayed. This cut off the flow of information in either direction.

Finally, this reduced everyone's stress. Laid-off employees didn't have to worry about looking their coworkers in the eyes while they pack their possessions, making it easy for them. A lot of management personnel were gone, making it easy on management and offloading the hard task to security personnel who didn't know laid-off employees personally. The executive performing the layoff had to stay. As a leader, he was responsible for this layoff and it was his duty to remain until the end.

I had another customer who followed the opposite strategy. He gathered a team of people in the conference room in the middle of the day. He then announced that business has been shrinking, and therefore he needs to let people go. Fortunately for them, these people were actually selected to stay. They were then asked to spend the next half an hour in the conference room while the laid-off staff was collecting their belongings. They were told it's a great idea because it will make it easier for the laid-off staff to not look at people who will remain with the firm. During this speech, another manager called the rest of the employees into another conference room and announced that they were getting laid off. They collected their belongings and left with no one around them to watch. This approach worked as great as the previous one.

But then there are layoffs that go totally wrong. I've seen one layoff in the Republic of Belarus where the factory manager simply announced to all employees that some of them are about to lose their jobs. They should come in the next day and look at the list of laid-off people posted on the board. If their name is on the list, they should report to HR to complete their exit paperwork. Everyone made it to HR to pick up their last pay.

After that, almost everyone went back to their work place to pick up an "exit gift" in the form of a machinery part or one of the company's products they could sell. Remaining employees decided to follow the "exit gift" strategy out of fear that they will be next to go and that the company will now be smart enough to prevent theft. Their "exit gifts" included everything from machinery parts to raw materials to a large television set from the factory cafeteria. Because the number of parts went missing from machinery, the factory stalled for weeks. This particular employer violated every objective we have listed. Employees were aggravated. They were allowed to stay on premises. They were able to communicate with those who stayed. They were able to find out which products the factory manager forgot to secure from theft. They stole items, creating an even bigger stress for the manager, who was eventually terminated for mishandling this layoff.

A layoff I've seen in the United States created theft simply by annoying the wrong people. A Fortune 500 company decided to lay off a few hundred staff working for a money-losing division. It announced that it was laying off engineers and marketing folks. The firm's information technology team was asked to supervise all security matters and then collect and inventory all equipment used by the departing staff. This team worked closely with people about to be laid off and felt very bad for them. They were allowed to spend some time talking and saying goodbye to each other but at the end were asked to do their jobs and collect and inventory all equipment. After equipment had been collected and inventoried, they were laid off themselves. These information technology folks were so annoyed with how it was handled that they took most of the inventoried equipment with them.

There are two other things you should remember when you design your walk-out process: culture and business processes or business model. For example, if your business involves seasonal hiring (e.g., a ski resort), your employees most likely expect to be laid off at some point after the season is over. Many employees working in U.S. retail take layoffs relatively easy, knowing they can get similar jobs within a day or so of losing their employment. Employees working in national defense expect to be walked out under strict supervision, which makes it normal. In countries like Japan, layoffs are so abnormal that employers implement "work-sharing" programs, slashing employees' hours and salaries and having them share each other's work in order to avoid letting them go. Alternatively, the Japanese implement early retirement programs and spend weeks convincing their staff to resign voluntarily. Russians are the exact opposite of the Japanese. While the Japanese believe that letting someone go is like disowning one's children, Russians cut personnel the same way they shoot ducks during the hunting season. The lack of equal employment opportunity laws allow Russians to easily cut people's jobs based on age, religion, gender, or the color of their eyes.

As you can see, the difference between the right and wrong walkout processes can make a huge difference. Design yours carefully. Take the aforementioned objectives, culture, and business process into consideration.

Theft Control

Whenever there are aggravations, there's potential for theft of company property. It doesn't matter how good employees are and how much the employer trusts them. When jobs are cut and aggravations come in, theft becomes a usual thing employees can justify in their heads. Consider the following example.

A Fortune 500 company was going through a small round of layoffs. After people had been let go, the firm noticed that it was missing some laptop computers. Finding them wasn't tough. People who these laptops were assigned to were contacted and asked to explain what happened to their equipment. While some of these employees played ignorant, others knew exactly what they did and justified theft with what they thought made absolutely perfect sense. Here are some responses the company collected.

I was the lowest-paid employee in the department but I did as much work as everyone else. I took the laptop because I needed something to compensate for the difference in pay.

I took it. I didn't steal it.

I didn't steal it. They just forgot to take it from me.

There was nothing in my offer letter stating I should return the laptop if I am terminated.

I am keeping the laptop. It's not my fault that I was laid off.

A reasonable person would probably state that these employees were delusional. Yet all of them were able to rationalize what they did to themselves. In most cases, these rationalizations came as a result of aggravations these employees had due to a mishandled layoff.

When protecting the company from theft, one should consider the following three types of assets.

Capital assets. These are material goods, such as computers and furniture.

Data. Many companies hold and maintain customer or other proprietary data.

Trade secrets. This is competitive information describing how certain things are done in your firm.

Each type of asset should have its own strategy for protection. Capital assets and data require up-front preparation. In other words, you should have protected them with internal security controls before layoffs even occurred. For example, some companies chain computers to desks, install surveillance cameras covering every part of the work area, or put antitheft devices on computer equipment. Data can obviously be protected with passwords. Access to data should be cut off before employees find out about layoffs.

Trade secrets are a little harder to protect. Some employers try to protect them by putting a clause in the employment contract stating that employees aren't to share trade secrets or work for competitors after termination of employment. While this may be a good idea, it is often hard to enforce. First, it may be hard to find out where your employees will go after they leave you. Second, courts in the United States are known to not enforce the so-called noncompete clause if employees can show that this clause significantly limits them in their job search, resulting in undue financial hardship. Some states even prohibit the use of the noncompete clause. That being said, there are many cases of the opposite as well. There is the famous case of Kai-Fu Lee, a Microsoft senior executive who joined Google, resulting in a multimillion-dollar lawsuit. But this noncompete clause may apply to rank-and-file employees as well. I've witnessed many cases like this. One that comes to mind is a case of a customer service representative who went to work for a competitor and was fired after the new employer was sued by the old employer for assisting this person in breaking the noncompete agreement.

The bottom line is that company assets shouldn't be ignored. Companies should develop processes and procedures to prevent theft of physical goods and data and consult their attorney on securing their trade secrets.

Legal Considerations

When employees are annoyed, lawsuits happen. Because lawsuits require money, most of them have merit. In fact, most employees either find lawyers who believe in the case and take it on a contingency basis or drop the case when they find out how much attorneys will charge. But there are cases of somewhat bizarre lawsuits. I've seen a case of an employee suing her employer for not giving her enough training to find the next job. I've also seen a case of an employee suing for wrongful termination because her offer letter didn't warn her of such possibility.

When the lawsuit is brought up, it costs money, regardless of whether or not it has merit or makes any logical sense. One study shows that average attorney fees for cases that go to trial are around $250,000 and $95,000 for cases that don't go to trial. This means that lawsuits should be avoided all together. There are two things employers can do to avoid lawsuits.

Reduce aggravations. Aggravations are why employees sue and do a lot of other crazy stuff, like steal. As noted earlier, you can reduce aggravations by treating people with respect, by treating them fairly and honestly, and by helping them.

Consult attorneys. Various countries, states, and provinces have laws applicable to terminations. It's impossible to list them all here, so companies should contact their attorneys for assistance. These laws may not make sense, but breaking them isn't a good idea either. For example, the Republic of Belarus requires employers to sign employment contracts with potential candidates listing an expiration date and prohibits them from terminating employees for any reason before such expiration. The United States has the Worker Adjustment and Retraining Notification

Act (WARN), requiring large employers to give employees a 60-day notice before major layoffs.

Avoiding lawsuits is important from several perspectives. Lawsuits can cause financial harm, destroy your brand, take up your time, and cause negative reactions from your remaining employees. Even when lawsuits look like a sure thing, they should be avoided as much as possible.

There is a school of thought that follows the opposite strategy as well. The idea is that if an employer responds to every single lawsuit and puts money into each one without ever agreeing to settle, employees will eventually learn that this employer isn't scared of lawsuits and will fight until the end, prompting employees not to sue. While this strategy may work sometimes, it also has flaws. First, it doesn't stop most lawsuits because they are driven by aggravations. In fact, nothing can stop people when they are annoyed. Second, it sends remaining employees a negative message, showing that their employer is ruthless and doesn't care. Some of those messages get out on the street. As a result, new potential candidates don't want to join the firm, and customers don't want to do business with the firm that does something negative to employees and then uses its financial might in court. Employers should definitely consult attorneys when making layoff decisions.

Let Others Know What Happened

Letting your remaining employees know what happened to the unlucky bunch is as important as, if not more important than, managing the layoff process of those who left. In fact, employees who remain have the power to do even more damage than those who left. They can damage your data, plant time bombs for when they will be let go, communicate competitive information to those laid off, or, even worse, go into a depressive mode that has consequences of its own. These employees may experience sharp performance degradation, lose motivation, search for work, and leave your firm. Loss of motivation and performance degradation may mean poor customer service and financial loss due to a deficit of productivity.

The news of the layoff may come to your remaining staff as a shock. When that happens, human nature dictates that they talk about it with each other. These conversations simply make them feel better. Such conversations start with theories and eventually turn into gossip. Human nature makes gossip almost uncontrollable. This gossip eventually turns into what employees perceive as truth. All decisions are then based on this false truth, which is rarely positive. Depending on what this truth is, employees can destroy your firm completely.

In order to prevent this from happening, employers should be prepared to communicate with remaining employees *immediately* after the layoff, before the rumor mill begins. Typically employees are looking for answers to the following three questions.

1. Why the lay off?
2. How were the specific people to be laid off selected?
3. What and when will happen with other people?

While it's important to be honest with remaining employees, these answers should be handled in a careful manner.

If you have a culture of transparency, you hopefully already communicated the answer to the first question before the layoff even occurred. If not, you should start now. People deserve to know what happened. They also deserve to know what you are doing to prevent future layoffs. Here's a sample speech you can give:

> As some of you know already know, we reported a $50-million loss in the last quarter due to our customers leaving us for our biggest competitor. As a result, we had to cut some of the staff. But we are not in the business of losing to competition. We don't want to cut any more staff. That's why our team came up with a turnaround strategy that will get us our customers back.

The second question should show people that this layoff wasn't totally random. Although it may not change the outcome, they like to know. It often makes people more comfortable knowing how you came up with your layoff list so that they see if they fit your criteria and may get laid off soon as well. One approach I've seen companies use is cut the bottom performing staff. Announcing that you cut the bottom 10% of your workforce makes your top performers feel better about their future.

The third question tells them what will happen next. What are the chances of them being let go? How soon? Again, what are you doing to prevent that? No matter how bad it may sound, the truth is usually the best answer here. How you present it will certainly make a difference.

There's one more component to what you say to your remaining staff: motivation. No matter the news, you should always find a way to get your company moving. Even if you deliver answers to the previous three questions, some people will lose motivation. You have to find a way to keep it.

Here's an example of a speech you can use. You should obviously derive yours from this one and not use it exactly.

I am sure some of you already heard that we had to let some people go. I want to be the first one to tell you that employees are our biggest asset, and it's very unfortunate to see them leave. I want to take full responsibility for what has happened. We've all been working as a team to stop our customers from leaving us for our biggest competitor, but we lost the first round. We reported a $50-million loss in the last quarter, resulting in a financial gap the firm just couldn't handle. But we are not in business of losing to competition. If we were to continue doing what we were doing, we'd probably file for bankruptcy and close our firm. But that's not why we are here. We'd like to save our firm, beat competition, and become the number-one provider of widgets in the world. In order for us to recover from the financial gap and meet our goals, we had to cut some of our staff. To select the people to let go, we carefully evaluated everyone's productivity and laid off folks with the worst productivity in the firm. That's right! These people represented the bottom 10% in our team that caused the problem in the first place. Moving forward, we don't want to cut any more staff. We learned our lessons and know how to beat our competition. Our team came up with what we believe is a winning strategy that will get us our customers back and put us back in the number-one spot. First, we'll match our competitors. We'll bundle our widgets with free warranty. Then, we'll beat our competitors. We'll offer deeper discounts and free extended warranty, which is possible due to our competitive cost structure. Our customers will come back to us! But I will need your help as well! In order to bring back our customers, we need to improve our level of customer service.

We want to be known as having the best customer service in the industry! I ask each and every one of you to think of ways we can improve customer service, our product, and our firm in general. Please submit your ideas directly to me. With this approach, we will prevent future layoffs and build a stronger company.

This speech answers all three questions and tries to add a dose of motivation. This motivation comes in the form of positive words, mentioning of teamwork, an explanation of what the firm is going to do, a call for action, and confirmation that this winning strategy will prevent future layoffs and do something great for the firm and its employees.

As mentioned earlier, a speech like this should be custom tailored to each firm and each situation. But no matter the situation, it should always answer the three questions listed previously and never leave employees in the state of the unknown. The more questions you answer for them, the less they'll guess. The less they guess, the less gossip they'll distribute. And gossip, as we know, is a powerful organizational destruction weapon.

Send the Right Message

Speaking to your employees isn't the only way of communicating. Whether you want it or not, employees watch your actions as much as they listen to your words. Your actions should obviously mimic your words. But sometimes it may not be as easy as it seems. In fact, it's not about what you meant to say with your actions, but what people actually heard.

Consider the following example. A CEO of a large firm flew down to one of his plants to shut it down. He gave a frank talk to his employees, stating that the firm was doing this to cut costs needed in order for the firm to stay profitable. He left, hoping his employees understood the reasons. But his employees saw a different picture. They saw a CEO fly a $60-million corporate jet to close down a plant that will save him $20 million a year. In their mind, selling the jet was a much better approach to cost cutting. They saw him as a greedy liar who cared about himself and his own executive perks rather than the lives of his own employees. Of course, using the corporate jet made perfect sense to this CEO. With a salary of $10 million per year, which translates into $4,800 per hour, he only spent an hour traveling that day instead of eight hours it would have taken him if he took commercial airliner. He spent the remaining seven hours in strategy and mergers and acquisitions (M&A) meetings that resulted in $100 million in value over the next year. In addition, this plane was a sunk cost and only cost $10 million after depreciation. It served a group of executives and saved the firm over $1 billion a year in opportunity costs. It only made sense to use it. But employees didn't see it that way. Lawsuits followed.

A more obvious example of such action is bonuses. Typically employees find it hard to justify layoffs if they are for any reasons other than to save the firm. If the firm has money to pay bonuses, employees believe they shouldn't be laid off. At the bare minimum, a lot of people believe it just isn't fair to be laid off while someone else gets a bonus. Yet many firms do just that and find good reasons to justify it. In most cases their justification makes sense, but just like in the case of private jets, it's not the justification that matters but what employees really think. Large diversified companies like GE and Procter & Gamble can easily lay off people in a line of business they would like to close and give large bonuses to people in a line of business that just turned a big profit. This makes perfect managerial sense and it makes sense to those receiving bonuses, but people losing their jobs don't want to hear it.

Messages like this can create a number of undesired effects, so they should definitely be avoided. While it's hard to do so, employers can run through a simulation exercise that helps them predict such messages.

To run through this exercise, take a group of 6–10 people and split them into two groups. Ask one group to represent the employer, and the other to represent the employees. The goal of the employer group is to convince the employees that it's good for them to lose their jobs. The goal of the employee group is to convince the employer to let them stay with the firm and to prove to the employer that the firm is laying them off on purpose in order to destroy their personal lives. Ask both sides to present their arguments as a monologue and then have a nonmoderated open discussion between both sides. Have a third party take notes. Although not always 100% effective, such exercises can reveal a number of things never considered by employers. To hear different results, try diversifying people on both sides. Go through this exercise with senior- and junior-level managers and then rank-and-file employees. It's amazing what you can learn!

The Aftermath

Depending on the size of the layoff, the reason behind it, and how it was handled, the consequences can be anywhere from minimal to devastating. Some employers try to help employees who just lost their jobs. While it can be good, sometimes doing nothing is better than doing something.

When people lose jobs, the biggest thing on their minds is how they'll get that next job. Unless you can help them answer that question, it's probably better if you don't contact them at all. Anything you do outside of their expectations may result in additional aggravations. Here are some examples of things employers like to do that they should not.

Don't send employees letters or flowers. Some employers like to send their employees flowers, balloons, or thank-you or good-luck letters. Any of those things can annoy people. Terminated employees try to forget their past employers and move on with their lives. The last thing they need is another reminder. Some employees find a way to create negative associations with such communication. For example, I've heard one employee say, "Oh, they don't have money to employ me but they have money to send me flowers! I'd rather have them send me money." It's highly recommended that you stop all communication with your past employees.[7]

Don't apologize. It's only human to apologize when you do something you feel bad about. But an apology can cost you a lawsuit. In fact, an apology may be taken as a sign of your recognition that you made a mistake. Courts are known to award financial judgments for mistakes. While most lawsuits arising out of apologies give employees a little bit of money just to cover the grief, some employees can even take it further and prove that it wasn't the manager's mistake for letting them go but the CEO's mistake for putting the firm in a condition resulting in downsizing. Such proof can result in major lawsuits.

Don't keep their hopes up. Giving employees hope is another concept humans like to use. Some employers are known to promise to rehire employees back if something comes up. While it's a nice gesture, it may result in a liability and additional aggravations. For example, your employees may interpret your conditional willingness to rehire as a definite promise and sue you if you don't hire them back. If they don't have money to sue, they'll get upset. As we already know, no one can predict or control people when they are upset.

Don't take any money from them. Some employees may owe you money. This can be a loan, a negative vacation balance, or money they owe you for any work-related activities. Don't take it away from them. When people lose jobs, the last thing they need is to have their debt mature immediately. This can create aggravations beyond belief and result in trouble for employers. I've experienced a case of an employee whose employer made a mistake and never deducted money from his paycheck to cover his health care benefits. When this employee was let go, his employer withdrew all money owed from the final paycheck, bringing it down to almost zero. Already in a poor financial situation and living paycheck to paycheck, this employee got upset and tried to turn his manager's life into hell. Claiming he didn't owe any money because it wasn't his fault it was missed in the first place, he called his manager numerous times day and night, threatened to sue, and then contacted remaining employees and told them what the firm did to him. The amount of money he owed wasn't worth the fight from the company's perspective. He ended up paying the company back, but the company paid more in manager's salaries while they were discussing the case than collecting from this employee.

As a good human being, you probably feel obligated to talk to your past employees. But unless you can give them financial assistance or help them find work, you should stay away from doing so as much as possible. Remember, any help you give them may turn into a liability.

CHAPTER 4

More Food for Thought

The Perfect Prescription

No, this book is not a perfect prescription. Nothing is. While I wanted this book to cover as much as possible, I can't cover every case. Even when you follow this book's advice, you should exercise great judgment and rely on your management skills to make the right decisions. Sometimes you may have to deviate from this guide, although such deviation should be an exception rather than the rule.[1]

The following few sections of the book are designed to give you some additional food for thought and address some more complex cases. While they are not all-inclusive, they may give you ideas for those hard-to-deal-with situations not listed here. Please note that sometimes there's no right or wrong way to handle a case, but there's usually a more effective way. This section isn't designed to provide you with *the* way but will address some cases that require special attention.

Do Some Research and Be Flexible

Because every case is different, it should be treated as such. Don't develop a single system consisting of one speech you give, one way to walk your people out, and one way you pay out severance pay. While you should have a general idea of how you want these things done, you should consider whether every part of the process applies to each instance of a firing or a layoff in the same way. For example, if your firm employs prison workers or individuals with disabilities, you may have to follow a different law to terminate them. If you have reason to believe that your employee will hurt you when you deliver candid feedback to him, fire him without giving him feedback or bring enough security detail with you when you deliver such feedback. If you are so dependent on your employee that ter-minating him or disclosing feedback may seriously jeopardize your busi-ness, find a potential replacement for him before you talk to him.

No matter the case, do some research, prepare your plan, and play through the scenario. Consider all possible outcomes. Go over your ter-mination process step by step and see whether each step applies. Consult your attorney for any adjustments to the process.

Verify all information given to you as termination justification. Believe it or not, some may be accidentally or maliciously misrepresented, result-ing in a wrongful termination. Ask questions. Verify all sources. Make an independent judgment. You may or may not agree with what was said.

I once had to terminate an employee for poor performance. His man-ager brought me a ton of justification showing how badly this employee was doing. However, after a very meticulous review, I realized that this employee was doing just fine. His performance wasn't a problem. The problem was that he just didn't click with his manager, resulting in this manager developing a negative bias toward this employee. This manager was coached and he understood the problem. But the employee never did. Further, the damage was so great on the employee's side that he didn't want to work with his manager anymore. He blamed the man-ager and refused to work things out. The manager was open-minded. The employee wasn't. This employee had to be let go. Although I had to terminate this employee anyway, I did so for the right reason. Had I used the wrong, biased reason, I could have gotten in legal trouble.

Golden Parachutes

Some companies establish a process called a golden parachute. This pro-cess creates a legal document binding the company to provide certain benefits to employees if they leave. For example, the firm may be required to pay severance if it lays off its employees. Large companies may create special golden parachutes for their senior executive teams. For example, when Bob Nardelli[2] left Home Depot, his golden parachute consisted of $210 million in cash and stock options, which included $20 million in severance pay and $32 million in retirement benefits. It didn't matter that Nardelli destroyed what Home Depot stood for. His golden parachute was only designed to attract him to come work for Home Depot in the first place.

While a golden parachute can be a great tool to attract talent, it can also be a way to destroy companies. Imagine trying to lay off people knowing that your severance pay may be greater than your cash reserves. Your people may not necessarily have hard times finding other jobs. You figure a 2-week severance pay is sufficient. Yet you end up paying 3 months' severance and cover other perks you promised to your folks when times were good and nothing seemed to stop your company's growth.

In late 1990s, the dot-coms in California were offering free BMWs as a sign-on bonus to software engineers. The terms of the offer were such that the employees were to buy their own cars and get 5-year car loans, with the company making monthly payments on those loans on behalf of employees. The thought was to use this strategy to attract talent and retain it for at least 5 years. When dot-coms started going out of business, they ended up with thousands of unpaid BMWs on their books with debt maturing immediately. These dot-coms thought they were smart by having employees take out their own car loans, hoping employees would continue making payments. Yet courts forced many of these dot-coms to cover the entire car cost based on employees' understanding that they get free cars when they accept job offers.

Whenever you make a decision to let people go, see how the golden parachute you set up may affect your actions. Obviously, if you need to terminate an employee for gross negligence, you would probably do so regardless of the substance of his parachute. But laying off may be a different story. You may find it less expensive to keep an employee on the bench, create a new position, or move him into a different job than let him go and then suffer the effects of the golden parachute. But don't let the golden parachute stop your actions either. A healthy balance can often be found. I know an individual who's been sitting in his job doing absolutely nothing for over 5 years. His golden parachute is so substantial that his boss doesn't want to approve laying him off. But staying in the job for over 5 years probably costs more than even the most generous golden parachute.

Always consider the effects of the golden parachute, but never allow it to dictate the rules. Always do what you think is right!

Golden Handcuffs

While golden parachutes provide for the well-being of terminated employees, golden handcuffs provide incentives for them to stay with the firm. The BMW example described in the previous section was one illustration. Other examples may include continuous bonuses, competitive health insurance and vacation benefits, free oil changes, access to tennis courts, free food, and so on. While things like free oil changes may not keep employees with the firm, free BMWs may. In fact, if employees leave on their own, they end up making the rest of the payments on their cars. Other such benefits may include expensive tuition reimbursements, mortgage subsidies, and corporate housing. If the firm pays $100,000 for an employee's executive MBA program, the employee is usually required to stick around for a year. Leaving early will require the employee to pay $100,000 back to the firm, which may be cost prohibitive. Leaving the firm providing corporate housing may be expensive too, since housing costs can make up one-third or so of your monthly income.

Thankfully, golden handcuffs aren't as financially demanding as golden parachutes. In fact, most employers can safely let their employees go and not be liable for any benefits offered, as long as they are willing to treat what they've spent thus far as sunk costs. For example, if the employer spent $100,000 on an executive MBA, it can't get it back. But the employer can safely forget about it and not owe any more money when it lets the employee go. The employer is also not liable for corporate housing, vacation, bonuses, free food, and tennis courts. They are all sunk costs that can be forgotten.

But employers should still consider the effects of some benefits. For example, in 2009 the United States passed a law requiring employers to cover a large portion of health insurance premiums for an extended period of time after the employee's termination, regardless of the termination reason.[3] Unemployment benefits may end up costing money as well, usually in the form of increased insurance premiums. Certain retirement benefits can present either financial or legal risk. For example, in the United States, if your employees have a retirement plan and you terminate them before paying out their retirement benefits, you may be found in violation of the Employee Retirement Income Security Act (ERISA).

You may also be found liable in some cases if you lay off your employees immediately before you pay out bonuses to the rest of your staff.

Although typically golden handcuffs don't represent any issues during termination, each employment contract and each set of benefits should be reviewed by the legal counsel to avoid any potential problems.

Voluntary Redundancy

Sometimes you need to lay off a group of people and you find it hard to select the unlucky bunch, especially if it's a strategic layoff rather than downsizing. Or you may find such a strong resistance from the union that a layoff may look impossible. In cases like this, companies use a concept called voluntary redundancy, which is essentially a financial incentive offered for the purpose of finding volunteers to leave the firm. This incentive is usually higher than severance offered in a regular layoff and is high enough for employees to take it without being forced to do so.

While voluntary redundancy is more humane than a layoff, it usually costs more money. When choosing between the two, companies should find a healthy balance between the costs and dealing with the aggravations of layoffs. Because layoffs may have a number of negative impacts on your firm and your brand, voluntary redundancy is a better choice. When voluntary redundancy is cost prohibitive, some companies design a strategy combining voluntary redundancy and a layoff.

For example, a firm may announce that it needs to lay off 1,000 people. It can then announce that it will pay 2 months' worth of salary to volunteers and 2 weeks' worth to those it will let go involuntarily. It will then ask for volunteers to quit. While most people won't find 2 months' worth of severance sufficient to quit their jobs, they will have to think about the risk of getting let go anyway and losing even the 2 months' worth. Some will quit, thinking they will get let go anyway. Others will stay, thinking they are the lucky bunch.

While this combination strategy may work in some cases, it carries many risks, most of them being negative. For example, courts in some countries may find such strategy to be discriminatory and require all terminated employees to be paid the same amount. Those who volunteered to leave probably did so under duress, since they thought they were going to get let go anyway. They won't feel that they were in control of the situation. Voluntary resignation won't feel any different to them than a layoff, except it may annoy them that they were forced into this set of circumstances.

As you can see, a mix of the two strategies can be dirtier than a simple layoff. Whenever possible, a pure, well-designed voluntary redundancy is recommended, but it should never be mixed with a layoff. The voluntary redundancy plan should provide enough benefits for employees to feel that they are making the right choice by quitting.

When Things Go Wrong

Not all terminations go well. While strategies described in this book are designed to minimize the number of potential problems, they only work with average, reasonable people. There are many people who these strategies will never work for. For example, people with mental disabilities or very poor listening skills may not be capable of understanding their situation or what hit them. Some people may not understand the technical background behind the layoff and still get deeply upset about it. People who easily lose their temper may get angry before you have a chance to handle the situation correctly. The bottom line is that sometimes you have to deviate from the rules and handle terminations differently.

I once had to help my client terminate an employee who had a problem with short-term memory. This employee was a recovered drug user whose brain cells were destroyed by several drug overdoses. He stopped taking drugs, but his brain was so damaged that he could only remember what had happened a few days ago. He couldn't remember what had happened 10 minutes ago or a few hours ago. When my customer sat down to talk to him about his performance, he realized their conversation wasn't going to go anywhere. By the time the manager got to his point, the employee forgot why he was there. This manager had to terminate the employee immediately without the employee ever understanding why. The employee went home. He showed up back at work the next morning as if nothing happened. He forgot that he was fired the day before. He was then told about a conversation from yesterday. He was shocked and went home. The next morning he was back at work again. Thankfully the manager only had to explain it to this poor employee one more time. The next day this employee called his manager in the morning and told him he now remembered their conversation from 3 days ago and wanted to confirm that his brain wasn't playing tricks with him.

Another interesting case I've seen was with a person who seemed to live in her own world. This is the same woman described in chapter 2 who filed the lawsuit because her coworker said hello to her. She was in her mid-40s when we met. She still lived with her mother and dated men who were at least 20 years younger than her. She refused to pay taxes simply because she didn't believe in doing so, resulting in constant problems with law enforcement officials. She openly invited a 20-year-old coworker out to dinner. When he refused, she filed a sexual harassment complaint against him with her employer, stating he was trying to force her to have sex with him. She was always late to work. When she did make it to work, she spent a lot of time in unproductive conversations with other employees, mostly complaining about her life. The only reason this employer kept her on the payroll is because she was an expert in a very rare field and this employer couldn't find a replacement for this individual. One day when she didn't show up for work yet again, her manager decided to let her go. Her manager called her cell phone and left a message. She then called the employee at home, and her mother stated that this employee had moved out of the house and into a hotel; the name and number of the hotel were provided. This manager then called the hotel only to find out that this employee has left all her belongings in the hotel and checked out a few days ago. The hotel representative was asking this manager what to do with all the belongings. The manager delegated finding this employee to a colleague. This colleague called the employee's cell phone and found her all well and supposedly at work. When the manager picked up the phone, this employee denied not being at work and claimed she was there all along and the manager was trying to set her up. When asked where she was right this second, she replied she was at her desk at work. Her manager was standing at that desk and did not see the employee. When presented with this fact, the employee insisted she was at her desk and the manager wasn't looking for her in the right place. Eventually this employee appeared at work about 5 hours late and claimed she was there all this time. When asked what she had done all day, she replied that she finished everything she was given to do. When asked for evidence, she replied that someone came in and destroyed it. This was an obvious case of lying and this employee had to be terminated. The challenge was that she was constantly in the defensive mode, and we already know that most conversations with people in the defensive mode are worthless. Her manager tried hard but couldn't explain anything to this employee. This employee seemed to have a justification for everything and she truly believed she was right.

If you follow an effective talent selection process, examples like this will be rare. But we are only human and can't predict all situations. I once had to fire a person with what looked like a dissociative identity disorder, more commonly known as split personality dissorder.[4] Just imagine interviewing one personality of the person and working with the other. Unfortunately, because of a negative personality change, I had to fire him, and his disorder made it such that he did not understand why.

Because situations like this can happen, managers should always have an *alternative termination strategy*. This strategy should describe an approach to terminating an employee when either something goes wrong during the normal termination process or when the normal process can't be applied. This alternative strategy can involve extra steps such as calling the police, escorting the person out of the building with extra security, or getting legal counsel involved. But managers should be careful when drafting such strategy. It may look discriminatory and result in legal action against the employer. Such a strategy will almost always guarantee that terminated employees will be annoyed. Preventing problems is hard in cases like this. Instead, employers should find a way to protect themselves and minimize the consequences of employee aggravations. Such consequences can include anything from lawsuits to physical assault, although the latter is rare.

Preventing lawsuits may or may not be hard, depending on your legal jurisdiction, the cause for termination, and the employee. For example, in most states in America, proper documentation presented to and signed by the employee will serve as enough evidence in court. Such documentation should make it clear that an employee was asked to do something and didn't do it or documentation must display gross misconduct. Consider the following example.

My client had to discipline an employee for poor performance. One of the reasons this employee's performance was poor was because he spent a lot of time conversing with other members of the staff. My client had several conversations with him but saw that they weren't going anywhere. This employee truly believed he was a megaproductive star and didn't agree that he spent too much time talking with others. His manager wrote up a document outlining the issue and stating that this employee had 30 days to improve his performance or he would be let go. The employee signed the document and then quit voluntarily a week later. He went to numerous lawyers trying to bring a lawsuit against his employer but no one wanted to take on the lawsuit because he signed a piece of paper stating he agreed to improve his performance. A single properly designed document was able to protect this employer from what could have been a costly litigation.

Unfortunately, the alternative termination strategy may be the only prescription against the some of your employees, although this should be an exception, rather than the rule. Because of the possible consequences, every step of the process should be designed in a way that prevents or minimizes problems. Consultation with the legal counsel is usually a required step.

But one should be careful when utilizing the alternative termination strategy and only apply it when all else fails. Too often managers utilize it because they assume their employees aren't capable of understanding why they are being terminated, while in reality these managers may not simply be capable of explaining the reasons. A lot of this comes from leadership. If employees don't understand, see if managers communicated properly. Time and again you may find that managers just didn't know how to deliver the message or they didn't feel comfortable doing so. In cases like this, try to prevent managers from using the alternative termination strategy and teach them how to do it right.

Laws, Laws, and More Laws

Every country and every state, province, and city has a set of laws designed to help either employers or employees. Some politicians are so worried about the well-being of their constituents that they totally forget the impact of their legislation on employers.

Unfortunately, this leaves employers in a state where every wrong move can be fatal. Some of these laws are very counterproductive, but breaking them may prove to be even costlier.

Consider the Family Medical Leave Act (FMLA) in the United States. Under this law, employees have a right to take unpaid leave for health related reasons or if they need to take care of a family member or attend a funeral. While the intent is great, many employees take advantage of it to the extent that it ruins the employer's productivity level. What makes it even harder is that employers can't terminate employees for poor productivity in such cases because they can be deemed as being in violation of the law.

Consider the following example. My client had to terminate an employee for poor work attendance, which seriously affected the company performance and ultimately resulted in degradation in the level of customer service. This employee only showed up at work 2–3 days a week. Every time she missed a day at work, she brought a note from the doctor stating she needed to stay at home due to having a migraine. Her manager overheard her say to another employee that her migraines weren't real and she was only using them as a way to skip work. Unfortunately, this manager had no proof. The employee couldn't be terminated because it would be in violation of the law. It got worse when this manager tried to terminate the employee for cause as well. An attorney reviewing the case concluded that any termination for any reason may look like a set-up in order to avoid compliance with the law and suggested this employee not be terminated for any reason. Eventually the employee was terminated when she threatened to hurt her supervisor. Thankfully, she didn't sue. However, she did file for unemployment, which she wasn't eligible for due to being terminated for cause. In the unemployment hearing, the mediator turned this case into a gray area when he announced that although this employee was terminated for cause and the decision to terminate was probably good, there was no evidence of real intent to hurt the supervisor and therefore this employee was eligible for unemployment. Had she taken this employer to court, she would probably have reasonable chances of winning by stating she was really fired for missing work.

Unfortunately, such examples aren't rare. There are many laws regulating employment. While most HR executives know them by heart, many managers terminating employees are ignorant of them. Consider the following examples.

1. A manager laid off a female employee after he found out she was pregnant. His thought was that he couldn't afford for her to go out on maternity leave so he wanted to replace her before she leaves. She sued for discrimination and won.

2. A manager fired an employee for poor performance, stating the employee was too slow. This employee sued for age discrimination. He stated in court that he was slow because of his age and everyone else in the firm who was fast was much younger than he was. Even though the employer responded that speed was essential to company operations, this employee won the case.

3. An employee was dismissed for refusing to follow company policies established by a senior executive. This employee sued, stating she was fired because she belonged to a political party other than the one of the senior executive. She proved it in court by showing that his policies looked similar to those that would typically be established by a person belonging to the Republican Party.[5] As a Democrat, she opposed such policies. She won the lawsuit.

4. An employee was laid off due to company downsizing. She sued the employer, stating she was promised lifelong employment during her job interview. The firm stated that employment "at will"[6] applied in this case and the firm had a right to terminate the employee any time for any reason. This employee won, however, because the court found that the implied-contract exception[7] applied to her because she was promised lifelong employment.

5. An employee called the police and complained that his colleague was performing an illegal act. The police investigation put the company on the first page of major newspapers, creating negative publicity for the firm. This company fired the whistleblower, alleging he destroyed the company. It stated that it could have used upper managers to resolve the issue in a more confidential way, in which case the firm would have survived. This employee sued and won under the premise that such termination violated the public policy of the state, which is to keep employment of people that do something for the public good.

All five examples listed above have one thing in common: the managers were ignorant of the laws. In order to avoid such pitfalls, companies can develop an approval process, whereby all terminations will first be approved by the legal counsel. Surprisingly and unfortunately, sometimes it may be more cost-effective to keep employees on the payroll than let them go.

But this doesn't mean unwanted employees should stay. In fact, keeping them would probably be considered poor management. Instead, companies should develop alternative strategies for letting people go. Fortunately, if you have a culture of candor, you have a good chance of explaining any issues to your employees and have them leave voluntarily.[8] If you don't have such luxury or if your employees aren't willing to quit, you have to design a reasonable solution together with your attorney. Such solutions are usually designed on a case-by-case basis. There's no formula that fits in every case.

Consider the following two examples.

1. My client had to fire an employee for poor performance. His attorney expressed a concern over the employee's race, stating that this termination may look like racial discrimination because the employee was a minority. To solve the problem, this employer first found a replacement employee who turned out to be a minority himself. Replacing a minority with another minority no longer looked like discrimination. The poor performer was now successfully fired.

2. A whistleblower reported to the customer that her employer was cheating on its invoices. Although the whistleblower was right, the problem turned out to be human error rather than conscious fraud. The firm fixed the problem and refunded any money owed to its customers. Meanwhile, the whistleblower had imagined that she couldn't be fired no matter what she did because it would violate the law. Her performance level came close to zero. Luckily, her employer found a remedy. The company announced a new process, publicly posting employee productivity numbers across this employee's department. It also announced that employees not meeting the quota would be terminated. The firm then spent the next 2 months posting results every single day. Every time the quota wasn't met, the company sent out a warning document to every employee who didn't meet it. The supervisor would then meet with employees who received a warning and coach them on improving their performance. At the end of the 2-month period, there were two people who didn't meet the quota. The whistleblower was one of them. Both people were terminated. Both received the same cause for termination and both were terminated the same way. The firm had 2 months' worth

of signed warnings and meeting notes. It showed that it followed a well-documented process. By firing one more person in addition to the whistleblower, it also showed that the whistleblower wasn't singled out and the policy applied to everyone.

As you can see, successful strategies can be developed. Be careful when you develop them, and make sure you consult a legal specialist in every single case.

Unions

Although the shifting nature of work and the mass introduction of knowledge workers[9] into the workforce in late 1990s reduced the number of union employees, it hasn't reduced unions' power. While unions created such widely used concepts as vacation days and weekends, they have at times also created unaffordable financial packages that put employers out of business. Airlines such as Delta and United were forced into bankruptcy in part by the demands of contracts negotiated with the unions. There are exceptions, of course. Southwest Airlines is completely unionized, but its employees are so motivated to help their employer that any union negotiations end up in positive relationships.

While no relationship can be predicted completely, there's one concept most union and management relationships have in common—rules for employee layoffs and terminations. In an effort to protect union jobs, unions support a number of rules regulating layoffs and firings. Some rules dictate that layoffs can never occur, or they can occur after the nonunionized workforce has been laid off first. Others outline a lengthy process, stating exactly what employers must do in order to let their personnel go. At times these rules are challenging or complex enough that employers must find alternative ways to achieve their goals while keeping employees on the payroll.

Some unions have contract stipulations requiring employers to only hire people who are already union members. Because such rules limit the supply of talent the company can employ, the firm is forced to limit the number of people it terminates, knowing that it may not be able to replace them once they are gone.

My friend who is a manager for a large multinational company told me a story about not being able to terminate her employee due to the employee's union membership. It turned out that the firm's contract with the union stated that employees can only be terminated once a year on a specific day in July, when the contract comes for renewal. The intent of such a clause in the contract was to force employers to make good judgment about employees as soon as they are hired. It was assumed that if it took the firm 6 months to make a firing decision, the firm didn't perform enough due diligence in the first place, making it the company's liability. The union would allow the firm to terminate an employee if the firm were to pay this employee severance up until the end of the contract. In my friend's case, it would have been 9 months' worth, which she couldn't afford. I spoke to my friend a month later and she still didn't have a solution.

The bottom line is that termination of unionized employees may sometimes be handled differently. Whenever you terminate a union member, check your union contract first. Consult your legal counsel and a union representative.

The Exit Management Process

You've learned lots of concepts in this book. Although these concepts can be acted upon individually, they are even more effective when implemented in a single system of processes, all communicating with each other. This system is responsible for effective talent management, which includes hiring, firing, and managing for performance. It's important to see how various pieces in the system interact with each other. For example, having a faulty hiring process may result in hiring the wrong people, ultimately impacting company performance. A deficient system of benefits or lack of employee motivation may result in employees leaving in droves, resulting in trouble for people doing the hiring. Concepts described in this book are individual pieces of the overall process, but they do impact other pieces as well. When designing your talent management system, do take these concepts into account and integrate them into the overall system.

An important part of the system managers rarely have in place is the exit management process. This process is responsible for managing employees' exit from the firm for any reason, whether it's termination or a layoff. This process should be integrated with the overall system and act as its integral part. The exit management process should consist of several steps that help the company meet the following goals.

Reasonably minimize costs. Of course the company should reduce costs. It's a good management decision and this may be the only reason for a layoff. But the word "reasonably" is key here. Squeezing every penny may not be worth it if it may cause negative consequences. For example, it may be worth it to hire a more expensive lawyer in order to reduce the chances of a lawsuit.

Minimize employee aggravations and their consequences. This book covers aggravations at length, especially for those employees who have been laid off. Consequences of aggravations may be anywhere from none to devastating. The exit management process should do everything possible to reduce these aggravations.

Protect the company and the brand. Terminations may cost money and aggravations may be unavoidable. But at the end of the day, it's all about protecting the company and what it stands for. Many companies manage to achieve this goal while minimizing lawsuits, theft, and other issues.

A well-designed exit management process should be able to take most cases into consideration. While covering every case is impossible, not covering it may prove fatal to the firm. Therefore, a firm must try to develop a catch-all process.

One of my clients found a way to do that by creating a special review process. This process would analyze risks associated with every layoff or termination and calculate the payment amount associated with letting employees go with minimum negative consequences. The firm found that by increasing its fringe rate[10] from 35% to 70% of the salary, it was able to cover every case, no matter the termination reason. It was a rather costly decision, but one the firm was willing to make.

There isn't a one-size-fits-all exit management process. Some companies have unions; others don't. Some companies have good leaders who know how to keep people; others don't. Some companies pay so well that no one wants to leave them; others are famous for negotiating the lowest salaries with their employees and managing employee turnover. Some firms have assets and knowledge to protect, while others have nothing confidential. Each company should design its own exit management process with its own business processes and requirements in mind.

Biases and Decision Making

Common sense is the collection of prejudices acquired by age eighteen.

—Albert Einstein

There are over six and a half billion people in this world representing six and a half billion opinions.[11] Each person grew up in his own environment and gained most of his knowledge from it. Each person's environment created a frame of reference for decision making. Each person takes this frame of reference as a given, calls it common sense, and makes all decisions based on it, believing he is right. It's hard to convince people that their frame of reference is wrong, but we still spend our lives proving our point to those who aren't willing to listen. Thus, a billion Christians will never convince a billion Muslims that one religion is truer than the other. Democrats will never convince Republicans that they are wrong either. People will often live and die with their beliefs. But these beliefs came from one single source: a frame of reference that was once placed by a set of events that occurred in one's life. For example, most people gained their religious beliefs from their parents. You don't see a lot of Christians born in Muslim families in Saudi Arabia.

Once we are born into families that force their beliefs on us and turn us into Christians or Jews, Democrats or Republicans, street drug dealers or successful career people, we start using these beliefs in everyday decision making, trying to force those beliefs on other people. It works sometimes, but then we come to work, and that's when we get in trouble.

Decision making in the workplace is one of the toughest things to do. We use our biases (which we call common sense or common knowledge) to make everyday decisions and get paid big bucks for it. But these decisions are driven by the same brain that is capable of believing in things two-thirds of the world doesn't believe in. These decisions are biased and they will be no matter what you do. While it's possible to reduce bias somewhat, it's impossible to get rid of it completely. After all, 100% of our knowledge is biased. Here's a fun example. Below is a list of statements with known facts that are usually taken for granted as real knowledge but are really false.

- A peanut is a nut.
- Tear gas is a type of gas.
- White chocolate is a type of chocolate.
- Arabic numerals came from the Arab world.
- Bananas grow on trees.

Most people accept these statements as common knowledge, but here's the truth. A peanut isn't a nut, but a legume. White chocolate is only called that but it isn't considered real chocolate by many people (including the U.S. government) due to the very low amount of cocoa solids it uses. Tear gas is solid. Arabic numerals came from India. Bananas grow on plants that look like trees but are technically herbs.

As you can see, common knowledge isn't always right. Yet we use our common knowledge to make everyday decisions at work. These decisions impact our companies and our employees. We also use such knowledge to make employee termination decisions.

One example of such knowledge is the belief that an employee's performance fully depends on the employee. The reality is that many, if not most, performance failures are solely due to management mistakes, such as placing people in the wrong jobs or not giving them enough direction.

Another mistake we make is when we use our knowledge about employees to make decisions in specific cases. We know our employees' tendencies and assume they always behave the same way. While it may generally be true, there are exceptions we should pay attention to but we don't.

Consider the following example. My client had an employee with poor communications skills. Let's call this employee "Jack" for the purpose of this example. The supervisor-employee communication became so bad that Jack's supervisor began to dismiss everything Jack would say or do. One day this supervisor received a complaint from another employee, let's call him "Bob," that Jack assaulted Bob and threatened to escort him out of the building. Jack went and purposefully undid everything Bob did, destroying weeks' worth of Bob's work. Jack's supervisor had enough. He decided to discipline Jack and started thinking about letting Jack go. This situation looked pretty bad. Jack didn't know how to communicate effectively, but now he was causing other employees to get upset with his actions as well. I thought this was a good case to research. I wanted to understand what Jack was thinking and where he was coming from, so I asked to speak with Jack. I was shocked when I talked to him. First, it turned out that Jack's communications skills weren't that bad after all. Jack was unique and required a different kind of management approach, but it was fairly doable. Second, his thinking actually made sense. My conversation with Jack sounded approximately like this.

> *Matt*: Jack, what do you think of Bob?
>
> *Jack*: I can't work with this nut! Can you believe what he did to me yesterday? He came into my office, sat down in front of my computer, opened my files, and started doing something. I asked him what he was doing. He responded that it's none of my business. I told him that if I find out he did something he wasn't supposed to do, I would personally escort him out of the building.
>
> *Matt*: Why did you undo all the work he just did?
>
> *Jack*: You know how everyone was complaining that our systems were down and no one could figure out why? Well, I figured it out. It's because of the changes Bob made. I just undid them and the system came back up.

This conversation presented the firm with a totally new viewpoint. Jack wasn't a liar. It turns out he'd been warning people about Bob for a while but his counsel had been dismissed. Because others saw Jack's communications skills as poor, they automatically assumed that everything he said was nonsense. But Jack was a smart man; he just didn't know how to get his message across effectively.

The firm ended up working all issues out with Bob and Jack. But people like Jack exist in every firm. What makes it even harder is when people like Jack become managers. They couldn't communicate with their superiors, but now they have to communicate with their subordinates. Because they are human, they make the same biased decisions as those who know how to communicate well. But in their case, the lack of communication creates such a strong bias that decisions often seem out of this world.

The moral of the story with Jack is that people make assumptions based on their biases and then make decisions based on those assumptions. This sounds dangerous, but that's how we govern the work-place, for we are only human and that's what we've learned to do in business school. What's worse is that we sometimes learn these management skills from our superiors or mentors who learned them from their own biased worlds, which don't always involve business school but definitely do involve a lot of bias.

We've built a collection of highly prejudiced human thoughts we call knowledge. We make decisions based on these thoughts and call our decision-making process management. When things go wrong, we refer back to our biased decisions and justify them with management again. This never ending sequence of biases creates a whole new world we live in that we love, respect, and take for granted. It makes sense to us, and that's what matters. The problem with this world is that we aren't alone in it; we share the planet but we only share some of the knowledge. When people disagree on the knowledge, they start wars, mismanage families, governments, and companies, and hire and fire the wrong people or for the wrong reason.

One can read this and state that he or she can be more open-minded in the future. It's definitely the way to go and everyone should try to do that. But remember, while it's a great start, it's definitely not the answer in every case. Unfortunately, it's impossible to remove all biases.

So what does this mean for the workplace and letting people go? Here's what you should do. When terminating people, try to review their story from a different angle. Put yourself in their shoes or the shoes of their coworkers or any other employees. Try to defend their viewpoints. Forget what you know or think about these people. Pretend you've never met. You may find out that things aren't really how they look. Develop a formal review process as a step in your exit management procedure. Ask others to perform an independent review of employees you wish to terminate. With the right decision-making process, you may find out that some people shouldn't be terminated while others, whom you've never thought about, should.

Exit Interviews

Many companies thrive by looking for and living through the "Aha!" moment. It's the moment that allows you to confront reality and define the general direction you need to head in. When done right, the "Aha!" moment comes with most biases filtered out. There are many ways to come to the "Aha!" moment, exit interviews being one of them.

The reality is that most employees are scared to speak the truth to their superiors. Some are scared of being punished; others just simply feel uncomfortable. Do you remember the last time your employee told you he or she was unhappy about you or something in the firm? Have you ever had an employee who quit and told you he or she was quitting because the employee was unhappy with you? Now consider the fact that 75% of the people quit because of their manager. Theoretically, this means that if you've never heard a leaving employee tell you he or she is leaving because of you, it means you didn't know the real reason for leaving in 75% of the cases, you've been potentially lied to in 75% of the cases, and you've missed many opportunities to learn about how you can improve yourself, your organization, and your communication and leadership skills.

What would you do if you could get every quitting employee to speak the truth, no matter how bad it sounds? Regardless of whether or not you agree with your employee, every piece of feedback can be valuable, as it may ultimately result in you being able to retain your employees in the future. Therefore employee feedback is critical!

One way to get your employees to open up is to conduct an exit interview. This interview must be performed by a well-trained person who is independent from your sphere of influence or at least your immediate surroundings. For example, a member of HR would probably do well, unless the quitting employee works for HR. A typical exit interview should only take a few minutes and be performed in a relaxed environment. An employee shouldn't be forced to attend and must feel comfortable talking. He or she should be invited directly by the interviewer. This is a personal conversation. Such conversations involve a lot of trust and require your employee to respect the interviewer and the interviewer to respect your employee.

Exit interviews should feel warm. When the exit interview starts, the interviewer should make the employee comfortable. It's a good idea to first thank the employee for everything he or she has done for the firm, unless the employee is being fired for some sort of offense, such as negligence, misconduct, or theft. It's also good to thank the employee for meeting with you.

The interviewer should try to make the questions as precise as possible, although it's a good idea to leave room for the employee to elaborate or sometimes go out on a tangent. One can think of variations of the same question. Your employee may or may not open up easily. Some employees may give you the whole story in response to a simple question of "Why are you leaving?" Most, however, will require some work.

The interviewer can start with general questions. For example, when interviewing an employee about his boss named Jane, one should ask the following questions.

- What do you think of working with Jane?
- How would you describe Jane's management style?
- What are Jane's strengths and weaknesses?

Some people may not answer the weaknesses part of the third question, so there's a different way to ask the same question:

Jane loves to receive feedback, but unfortunately she doesn't get any from her staff. If you could suggest one thing Jane could do better, what would you say?

About 50% of the people open up when they get this question. They may not think of weaknesses, but they can think of things that bother them about Jane.

If general questions aren't fruitful, the interviewer can try some more specific questions:

- What do you think of Jane's communication skills?
- How does Jane treat her employees?

The interviewer can also try to go into specifics:

- Can you think of an instance when Jane didn't treat you well?
- Would you mind giving me an example of Jane not leading by example?

Once the interviewer is done discussing the manager, he or she can ask the same questions about the company:

- What do you think of our benefits?
- What do you think of our work environment?

Then the interviewer should ask questions about the employee's fit with the firm. There's a good chance that this is why the employee is leaving. Here the interviewer needs to be a little bit more specific. He or she should first probe the employee's wants:

- What drew you to this firm in the first place?
- What did you expect from this job?
- What is your perfect job?

The interviewer should then ask whether or not the employee got what he or she wanted:

- You mentioned you were seeking challenge. Did you think your job with our firm was challenging? If not, what can make it more challenging?
- You mentioned that your perfect job involves working no more than 8 hours a day. What kind of hours did you normally work?

For every answer received, the interviewer should ask follow-up questions in order to draw a better picture of the situation. It is the interviewer's job to understand the entire nature of feedback and where the employee is coming from.

The interviewer should conclude the dialogue with an open-ended question:

- Is there anything else you'd like to tell me that we haven't discussed?
- Can you give us any advice on how we can improve our organization as a whole?

In most cases, employees already gave you enough information by the time you got to this final question. Yet some employees have only begun to talk when this question is asked.

Once you collect the feedback from your exit interview, you need to analyze it. Before you do so, remember the fact that your employees didn't want to give it to you directly; they gave it to an independent third party. There's a reason for that. Your employees know you well; they could have probably predicted your response when you received feedback and that's why they were afraid of giving it to you. Now that you finally have this feedback, it is your job to not respond in the way your employees thought you would. Don't dismiss it. Try to understand where your former employees are coming from. Remember, their frame of reference is different from yours. You need to understand it. Use the interviewer to explain it to you or help you understand the big picture.

I remember conducting an exit interview for a senior manager. This manager was just promoted into his position a few months before he quit. His boss was terribly upset, stating he lost a lot of time and money by promoting this manager. The quitting employee told him he was leaving because he received an offer for a dream job with the government. It all sounded good, but the exit interview revealed a few things. It went approximately like this:

Matt: Lou, can you tell me why you are leaving?

Lou: Yes, I've explained to my boss. I want to work for the government.

Matt: I saw you were promoted to your new position a few months ago. What did you think about it?

Lou (smiling): My boss assumed I wanted the job. I was never interested in this promotion.

Matt: Really? Do you think he understood that?

Lou: I tried to explain it to him but he didn't listen. He just simply went ahead and promoted me.

Matt: Do you think he didn't understand or he just didn't listen to you?

Lou: I don't think he understood. I know he heard me.

After the conversation, I called Lou's manager to get his side of the story. It went approximately like this:

Matt: John, what did you think of Lou?

John: I am deeply upset with him. I gave him a management job and he quit. He let me down.

Matt: Oh, what did he think about the new job?

John: He loved it!

Matt: What makes you think so?

John: Because he did a great job!

Matt: Do you think he even wanted it in the first place?

John: What kind of a person doesn't want to be a manager? But then, it doesn't matter. He is a professional and I am his boss. I decide what he will do.

Matt: Did he ever give you any indication that he didn't want the job?

John: No.

These two conversations went on and on and I collected a lot of more data about it. When I put together the two stories, I drew a clearer picture. The manager never listened to any of his employees. He always thought of himself being a decision maker. Any questions, concerns, or objections were immediately dismissed by him as excuses. His world was the right world. Everyone else couldn't be taken seriously. All overachievers were taken for granted and labeled as "just doing their jobs," while the rest of the staff was labeled as "incompetent."

As you can see, collecting and providing feedback isn't enough. It needs to be analyzed in a way that removes bias as much as possible and draws a clearer picture.

In general, when conducted properly, exit interviews can serve as great tools for improving people and the firm. They should be implemented as a part of the overall exit management or talent management process. The only time they shouldn't be used is when terminations are heated.

The Global Enterprise

The hot, flat, and crowded world[12] created a huge impact on the way companies do business. While China was once considered a place to manufacture products, it is now one of the biggest consumers of every imaginable good. Whereas 50 years ago most Fortune 500 companies were based in the United States, today many of them are headquartered in places like India, China, Singapore, and Taiwan. People change their spending habits. Many believe that a green car is far more important than a cost-effective one.

Companies constantly reinvent themselves. Local supply chains become global. Some multinationals sell in every market imaginable. This also means having to hire, retain, and fire talent globally. No longer can companies have a one-size-fits-all talent management strategy. The famous "think globally, act locally" cliché is now the strategic direction of every firm. This cliché applies to much more than products and markets. It also covers talent. In fact, hiring, motivating, retaining, and firing people in the United States is very different from doing so in Japan. In order to be effective, companies must focus their talent management efforts in each respective locale that will house its staff. While firms can often set the overall vision and define the mission for the entire firm globally, it's hard for them to find a common approach to staff motivation. It's also hard to centralize compliance with the law and develop processes and procedures for finding talent and for letting people go.

By thinking locally, companies can develop strategies that are unique to each geographic area. For example, the Japanese value long-term employment; networking and family environment mean a lot. Hiring people for a 1-year project or a high-risk assignment in Japan is very tough. In Russia, the concept of discrimination is close to nonexistent; it's culturally and legally OK to not hire people because of their nationality, gender, age, or religious preferences. The French value benefits such as long vacations; they don't want to work overtime and American notions of customer service don't fit well with their perspectives.[13] When Disney opened its Euro Disney park just outside of Paris, the company found it impossible to find people whose work ethic and values matched those of the Disney Corporation. People didn't want to work overtime. No one cared to give customers the fake smiles Americans are so used to. Workers were indifferent to customers. Employees didn't believe in their employer or their work. They just wanted to make money and go home at the end of the day.[14] Challenges like this may occur anywhere on the planet. Therefore, it's important to hire local managers and listen to them. They are experts in local talent. They can tell you what to expect. These managers should also be consulted any time employees must be terminated.

Of course, they can apply most of what you will find in this book, but they will also give you a lot of local insight this book doesn't cover.

Although the corporate talent management process should take local culture, laws, tradition, and processes into consideration, it shouldn't necessarily delegate 100% of talent management to individual regional teams. It may be OK if your company is already decentralized. But centralized management should never be replaced entirely with local processes. It should instead be complemented by them. A good process defines the mission and the overall approach to talent management. It may address such things as giving employees great benefits, creating a great working environment, building leaders, valuing customer service and loyalty, using the same talent management software, and any other things that may be valid across the board. But this process should also refer to regional decision makers on things that can make a difference locally. For example, choosing which schools to hire people from, figuring out what motivates employees, and what laws may apply to hiring or firing should be decided on a local level.

One of the hardest things to manage in a global organization is layoffs. A company can make a decision to cut 10,000 people across the board to reduce costs. It may sound like a good management decision, but consequences may be a little harder to manage. Layoffs are a way of life in Swaziland, are considered unwanted but normal in the United States, and are heavily frowned upon in Japan and Iceland. A centralized decision to lay off personnel can therefore have a number of unwanted consequences.

One of my clients decided to cut 10% of his worst performing staff across the board. He did just fine in the United States but got hit with heavy government fines in one of his offices in Eastern Europe. Right before the cut, he was rated as one of the best companies to work for in a little town in Eastern Europe; people were competing to come work for him. Immediately following the layoff, the candidate pool completely disappeared. No one wanted to work for a company that did such a "horrible thing" to its employees. My client's mistake wasn't that he decided to cut staff but that he didn't consult local managers before doing so. At least they would have advised him on proper procedures.

The bottom line is that enterprises must localize many processes dealing with terminations.

Conclusion

Layoffs and terminations must be done right. While there's no recipe that works 100% of the time, there is a set of actionable strategies one can follow to minimize any negative consequences. This strategy heavily depends on leadership, execution, analysis, being able to confront reality, having great general management skills, and being open-minded. This job cannot always be executed successfully by one person alone. It usually requires a whole new exit management process tightly entwined in the overall talent management process and introduced throughout the entire organization.

Notes

Chapter 1

1. Frugal Dad. (2008, September 8). Living paycheck to paycheck [Web log post]. Retrieved from http://frugaldad.com/2008/09/09/half-of-us-are-living-paycheck-to-paycheck

2. ISO 9001 is an international standard for managing quality. Please see http://www.iso.org for more information.

3. It is important to consider the legal distinction between employees and independent contractors and how they are treated. Please see U.S. Internal Revenue Service. (2010, August 3). Independent Contractor (Self-Employed) or Employee? Retrieved from http://www.irs.gov/businesses/small/article/0,,id=99921,00.html for more information on determining whether a consultant should be considered an employee.

Chapter 2

1. Sims, H., & Manz, C. (2001). *The new superleadership: Leading others to lead themselves.* San Francisco, CA: Berrett-Koehler Publishers.

2. Branham, L. (2005). *The 7 hidden reasons employees leave: How to recognize the subtle signs and act before it's too late.* New York, NY: AMACOM.

3. Ray, B. (2006, December 4). Who's afraid of the big bad boss? *FSU News.* Retrieved from http://www.fsu.edu/news/2006/12/04/bad.boss

4. Branham, L. (2005). *The 7 hidden reasons employees leave: How to recognize the subtle signs and act before it's too late.* New York, NY: AMACOM.

5. In fact, a survey conducted by my firm shows that most prospective employees only differentiate employers by the salary being offered. Things such as vacation, 401K, health and dental insurance, the work environment, and future potential are usually taken for granted or not considered at all. This is also confirmed by the Herzberg theory. The Herzberg theory states that employees take a lot of things for granted and don't see value in them. For example, employees expect things like vacation, holidays, and sick leave. If people compare two employers, they compare things that matter to them, like a salary being offered, but they often ignore things they normally take for granted, such as benefits.

6. Skarlicki, D. P., Ellard, J. H., & Kelln, B. R. C. (1998). Third-party perceptions of a layoff: Procedural, derogation, and retributive aspects of justice. *Journal of Applied Psychology, 83*(1), 119–127.

7. Refers to a set of incidents that occurred between 1982 and 1997, where U.S. postal service workers were killing their coworkers and members of the public due to stress incurred at the workplace.

8. This speech has been derived from an article published by Encina, G. B. (1999). Firing with dignity. Davis: University of California, Gregorio Billikopf Agricultural Extension. Retrieved from http://www.cnr.berkeley.edu/ucce50/ ag-labor/7article/article19.htm

9. The Kirton Adaptive Innovative (KAI) test measures the level of adaptability and innovation of the person. It can be used to determine which jobs are closely aligned with employee's personality.

10. Laurence J. Peter published a book in 1969 called *The Peter Principle*, where he stated that "in a hierarchy every employee tends to rise to his level of incompetence."

11. Security clearance is a status granting an employee access to very sensitive materials, sometimes involving matters of national security.

12. Defamation versus negligent referral is the policy of giving only basic employee references may lead to liability. More information is available at McCord, L. (1999). Defamation vs. negligent referral: A policy of giving only basic employee references may lead to liability. *Graziadio Business Report, 2*(2). Retrieved from http://gbr.pepperdine.edu/992/referral.html

13. Sun Tzu was a Chinese general who wrote *The Art of War*, a popular text on strategy and leadership.

14. For legal advice, see Niznik, J. S. (n.d.). What legal recourse do I have for employment-related defamation? *About.com*. Retrieved from http://jobsearchtech .about.com/cs/labor_laws_2/a/defamation_2.htm; or Reuters. (2005, August 23). Maris family, Anheuser-Busch settle multibillion-dollar suit. *USA Today*. Retrieved from http://www.usatoday.com/money/industries/food/2005-08-23 -maris-bud_x.htm

15. Some engineers are known to set up a way for their system to fail in the future, requiring their expertise to bring the system back up. They believe it will serve as the punishment to their employer if they were to ever get fired.

16. In the United States and many other countries, salaried employees (also known as professionals) are expected to work as many hours as it takes to get the work done. These people are usually paid higher salaries than hourly workers but aren't usually paid overtime.

17. See the section called "Having the Firing Conversation" in chapter 2.

Chapter 3

1. Frugal Dad. (2008, September 8). Living paycheck to paycheck [Web log post]. Retrieved from http://frugaldad.com/2008/09/09/half-of-us-are-living -paycheck-to-paycheck

2. The same study done by CareerBuilder.com claims that 21% of people earning over $100,000 per year also live paycheck to paycheck.

3. Cascio, W. F. (1993). Downsizing: What do we know? What have we learned? *Academy of Management Executive, 7*(1), 95–104; Datta, D. K., Guthrie, J. P., Basuil, D., & Pandey, A. (2010). Causes and effects of employee downsizing: A review and synthesis. *Journal of Management, 36,* 281–348.

4. Datta, D. K., Guthrie, J. P., Basuil, D., & Pandey, A. (2010). Causes and effects of employee downsizing: A review and synthesis. *Journal of Management, 36,* 281–348. Konovsky, M. A., & Brockner, J. (1993). Managing victim and survivor layoff reactions: A procedural justice perspective. In R. Cropanzano (Ed.), *Justice in the workplace: Approaching fairness in human resource management* (pp. 133–153). Hillsdale, NJ: Lawrence Erlbaum Associates; Skarlicki, D. P., Barclay, L. J., & Pugh, S. D. (2008). When explanations for layoffs are not enough: Employer's integrity as a moderator of the relationship between informational justice and retaliation. *Journal of Occupational and Organizational Psychology, 81*(1), 123–146. Trevor, C. O., & Nyberg, A. J. (2008). Keeping your headcount when all about you are losing theirs: Downsizing, voluntary turnover rates, and the moderating role of HR practices. *Academy of Management Journal, 51*(2), 259–276.

5. SWOT stands for "strengths, weaknesses, opportunities, and threats."

6. Porter's Five Forces is a framework for industry analysis designed by Harvard University professor Michael E. Porter. Please see Porter, M. (2009). How competitive forces shape strategy. *Harvard Business Review.*

7. There is, however, research that shows the contrary. For example, if some of those downsized are people you would like to rehire when or if the economy turns, then you may want to remain in contact with them. Just keep in mind that excessive contact with these employees may aggravate them. Play it by ear when making a decision to contact them.

Chapter 4

1. For example, if you start a new job and you have to fire someone your first day there, your employee may not necessarily know where he stands; you may just have to shock him and deal with the consequences.

2. Named one of the "worst American CEOs of all time," Bob Nardelli served as CEO of GE Power Systems, CEO of Home Depot, and CEO of Chrysler. Portfolio.com. (2009, April 30). Portfolio's worst American CEOs of all time. Retrieved from http://www.cnbc.com/id/30502091/Portfolio_s _Worst_American_CEOs_of_All_Time

3. The law actually states that it's the government that will pay 65% of COBRA premiums, but there are exceptions requiring employers to pay.

4. A person with this psychiatric condition may subconsciously show signs of having two or more completely distinct personalities.

5. In the United States, the Republican Party is one of the two most popular political parties.

6. Employment "at will" is a U.S. law that applies to all 50 states. It states that both employers and employees have a right to terminate employment any time for any reason without any liabilities to each other.

7. The implied-contract exception is the exception to the "at will" employment law, stating that all employment terms implied by the employer have to be met even when employment is "at will." An employment handbook is a good example.

8. Be careful with how you do this. In some states in the United States, asking people if they would voluntarily leave may be treated as constructive discharge and be handled as wrongful termination.

9. Knowledge workers in today's workforce are individuals who are valued for their ability to interpret information within a specific subject area. For more information, please see Drucker, P. F. (1973). *Management: Tasks, responsibilities, practices*. New York, NY: Harper and Row.

10. In many countries, the fringe rate is a percentage of the employee salary that goes to cover various employment benefits, such as vacation time and health insurance.

11. According to data published by World Bank there were 6.7 billion people in the world in 2008.

12. Friedman, T. (2008). *Hot, flat, and crowded: Why we need a green revolution and how it can renew America*. New York, NY: Farrar, Straus and Giroux. In his book, Friedman calls the world "flat," pointing out forces of globalization. He also calls it "hot" and "crowded" to point out forces of global warming and what companies do to make their businesses green.

13. Ask a Frenchman. (2009, August 21). Can you tell us about French customer service? [Web log post]. Retrieved from http://askafrenchman.blogspot.com/2009/08/can-you-tell-us-about-french-customer.html

14. Aswathappa, K., & Dash, S. (2008). *International human resource management: Text and cases*. New Delhi, India: Tata McGraw-Hill; Lau, G. (2009). *Business case study: The venture of Euro Disney*. Workshop presented at the Future Business Leaders of America/Phi Beta Lambda National Leadership Conference, Anaheim, CA. Retrieved from http://www.fbla-pbl.org/docs/NationalOfficerArea/TheVentureofEuroDisney.doc

Index